Ministry Endorsements for *The Milk and Honey Man*

Mr. Troth has done an excellent job of comparing the pilgrimage of the believer's spiritual growth to that of the children of Israel. I believe that a depth of understanding by the serious Bible student will result in spiritual growth of miraculous proportions as the Holy Spirit illuminates biblical truth.

—Dr. Charles R. Solomon
President and founder, Grace Fellowship International, Tennessee

The message of *The Milk and Honey Man* is so needed by God's people today. The insights give valuable teaching about our identity as believers and give directions in living in Christ's victory. Bill Troth has given the body of Christ a gift with this book, one of the most extensive treatments I have ever seen on the lessons from Israel's experiences from Egypt to the Promised Land.

—Dr. John Best
Director of Research and Exposition, Exchanged Life Ministries, Texas

It has been my privilege to know Bill and his wonderful wife, Helene, for almost three decades. I recognize a brother who consistently has lived a life that reflects the spiritual lessons that he has included in *The Milk and Honey Man*. While the Bible does use types to illustrate shadows or illustrations of concepts, they require great care in the application of biblical material. While I might not use that interpretative tool as extensively, I found sound and careful application for this very readable discipleship manual. *The Milk and Honey Man* takes the reader deep into the pages of the Bible. It is worth reading for the thought provoking examples that lead to mature Christian living.

—Dr. Tuvya Zaretsky
Director of staff development, Jews for Jesus, Los Angeles

I have known William and his family for more than two decades. *The Milk and Honey Man* is not only the story of the Israelites as they were led by Moses, but it is also the spiritual story of Bill and his wife, Helene, as they have been led by God throughout their lives.

The parallels that Bill identifies in *The Milk and Honey Man* between the typology of the Old Testament as related by Paul in 1 Corinthians 10, with our own walk, first, as natural men and women in the "Egypt" of our lives, then, as saved but carnal Christians as we roam in the "wilderness," and, finally, as spiritual sons and daughters of God residing in the "Land of Milk and Honey" and en route to a full life in Christ. Taking us from slavery to spirituality, Bill walks us step by step through bondage to sin, then saved but still subject to our carnality, and finally commencing our journey to the Promised Land.

If there were a contest for the rewriting of John Bunyan's *Pilgrim's Progress* as a non-allegorical work, William Troth's *The Milk and Honey Man* would win hands down. And Bill would give all the glory to His Creator.

—Ken Godevenos
President, SCA International, Toronto, Canada

This is a refreshing and challenging book. Bill Troth emphasizes that just as God's purpose in bringing His people out of slavery to Pharaoh was to bring them into the Promised Land—the land described as flowing with milk and honey—His purpose in bringing us out of slavery to Satan and the world system was to bring us into the peace, purpose, joy, and fullness of His indwelling presence!

The Milk and Honey Man will serve pastors well as a tool to communicate the message of the Christ as our life to their congregation. It would be tragic for anyone to miss out on His best for us here and now. Let us go on to maturity, not missing the Sabbath rest He has prepared for His people.

—Bill Fagan
Director, Discovery Foundation, Southeast Louisiana

Many Christians struggle due to the lack of knowledge. *The Milk and Honey Man* focuses on how to help the believer walk in true victory by resting in Him (Canaan land). I believe this book is a tool to help Christians dig deeper to find more gold so they can increase their spiritual knowledge. Teachers of the Word will find *The Milk and Honey Man* a great resource for understanding that what happened to the children of Israel was written for us.

—Leroy B. Herring
Director, Crossway Ministries, Decatur, Alabama

In *The Milk and Honey Man,* Mr. Troth has traced the development of God's people from bondage in Egypt to entry into the land of milk and honey. He shows how their pilgrimage parallels ours. This brings us to the abundant, victorious, Christian life that is filled with joy and peace as promised in the Word of God (Ps. 16:11; Isa. 55:12; John 10:10).

Just as the written Word of God is honey to the soul of a believer, so, too, the life of Christ lived through a believer is honey for him. "The righteous man shall live by faith" (Rom. 1:17) and when he does he experiences the sweetness of the life for which we were designed. And this sweetness is not for his own blessing and enjoyment. The greatest blessing of a believer's life is not that he receives a blessing, but that he *be* a blessing.

This book provides excellent guidelines and principles for moving toward becoming the Milk and Honey Man for his own blessing and abundant life and also for the blessing of people around him.

—Dr. Imanuel G. Christian
Missionary to his homeland of India and author of several
Bible commentaries in the Gujarati language of India

Pastoral Endorsements for *The Milk and Honey Man*

Bill Troth has done a great service to the Christian community in drawing attention to the importance of the Old Testament foundation for our faith in the types, or pictures, which are so crucial to a correct understanding of the great themes of Scripture. This book will lead the reader to the true meaning of the children of Israel and the application of their experiences to the modern Christian experience. The emphasis of the faith-rest or Christ-as-life concept is most helpful and refreshing.

—Pastor Joe Holmes
Senior pastor, Vestavia Hills Baptist Church, Decatur, Alabama

I appreciate Bill Troth's passion to see Christians continue to progress in their Christian journey. *The Milk and Honey Man* is both a source of encouragement and a road map to a deeper life with Christ. As you study Israel's transformation from slavery to possessing conquerors, I believe you will identify with your own growth as a truly devoted follower of Christ.

—Pastor George H. Sawyer
Senior pastor, Calvary Assembly of God, Decatur, Alabama

Whether you have studied the Bible for years, or you are just now considering reading the Bible for the first time, *The Milk and Honey Man* will be a blessing in your journey! Bill does a masterful job of explaining sin and grace in a very understandable way. His uses of charts and maps to bring the Old and New Testament together for present day application are obviously a result of decades of walking with God.

As a Lutheran Christian I would speak more of baptism's saving power, but even there *The Milk and Honey Man* speaks very powerfully about our connection to the death and resurrection of Jesus in baptism! Read, enjoy, learn, grow, and be blessed in what happened to them, but was written for us.

—Pastor Eddie Scheler
St. Paul's Lutheran Church, Decatur, Alabama

I appreciate the emphasis on typology in *The Milk and Honey Man*. The church of the twenty-first century hears very little preaching on types and symbols. Types and symbols are numerous in the Bible and ought to be given a fair emphasis in the interpretation of Scripture. *The Milk and Honey Man* is a good introduction to the study of types and symbols.

—Pastor Myron Mooney
Trinity Free Presbyterian Church, Trinity, Alabama

The Milk and Honey Man is loaded with typology that helps us understand the Israelites and their many years in the wilderness. It reflects on the trials and events that they faced and brings them to current day life application. Simple diagrams and chronological maps unveil the simplicity of all God wants us to have, and already have. God wants us to enjoy our lives in Him as we drink the milk and eat the honey, resting in Him.

—Pastor Barry Sempsrott
Austinville Church of God, Decatur, Alabama

To Debi
God bless you
Bill Troth
Gal 2:20

The Milk AND Honey Man

The Milk AND Honey Man

Happened to them...

written for us.

Now these
things happened
to them as an
example and
they are written
for our
instruction.
1 Corinthians 10:11

WILLIAM A. TROTH

WinePressPublishing
Your Book, Defined.

ISBN 13: 978-1-60615-064-1
ISBN 10: 1-60615-064-2
Library of Congress Catalog Card Number: 2010930533

To my wonderful wife, Helene Arzana Martin Troth. She is my pilgrimage partner of fifty years, the bearer of two wonderful children, and the grandmother of five wonderful grandchildren.

Two are better than one because they have a good return for their labor.
—Eccl. 4:9

The grass withers, the flower fades, But the word of our God stands forever.
—Isa. 40:8

List of Graphics

Contents

Acknowledgments

MY THANKS AND appreciation are directed to:

Bill Fagan, for sending me to the Exchanged Life Conference and sending me lots of Christ-as-life type books.

Rick Troth, for his encouragement. He said, "Dad, write"—more than once.

Helene Troth, Ken Godevenos, Robert Bumpus, Joseph Swanson, Olivia Brannon, Dr. Bennie Nobles, and Jon Tucker, for their work in proofreading this book. Many of those who were asked to read the book with the prospect of endorsing it also offered many helpful corrections and suggestions.

The First Bible Church Carpenters' Adult Bible Fellowship, who had no idea they were contributing to the development of a book.

Leroy Herring and the Thursday morning Bible study at the Gospel Lighthouse, who tolerated my oppositional thinking.

Dr. Reggie Gladish and the men of the Wednesday night Bible study, who also were patient with me.

Martin Troth, for graphics on the make-up of man.

Joel McWhorter, for development of graphics and design of the book cover.

And, again, to all who graciously took the time to read the book with an eye toward endorsing it.

Foreword

The Disciple and Eating Honey

WHILE GROWING UP in a small village in India, my older brother and I used to roam for hours in the farms and fields, sometimes collecting fallen mangoes from under the mango trees and sometimes collecting firewood in the forest. Many times, especially while collecting firewood, we would come across a small honeycomb. We would shake the branch to shake away all the bees and then grab the comb and eat honey directly from the comb. The taste was so different from the bottled honey we can get in a grocery store today—it was chewy and sweet and its flavor stayed with you for a long time.

Recently I was reminded of that sweet experience while reading a portion of the Scripture. Did you know that the Bible advises us to eat honey, honey from the comb? Proverbs 24:13 says, "My son, eat honey, for it is good, Yes, the honey from the comb is sweet to your taste." It even speaks of eating "honey from the comb." What I did as a boy growing up in rural India is a very commonplace experience of every boy growing up in those environments. Similarly, it was, and most probably still is, a very commonplace experience for the people in the Bible land. For example, Jonathan poked his staff into a honeycomb and licked some honey (1 Sam. 14:27). Samson, while walking on a trail through the wilderness, found honeycomb in a dead lion's carcass and picked up the comb and ate it (Judg. 14:8–9). In the New Testament wild honey was a part of John the Baptist's diet.

Honey in Israel was considered something special and was a symbol of the best and most satisfying food. When someone went to visit an important person he would take honey as a special gift to honor that person (Gen. 43:11; 1 Kings 14:3; 2 Sam. 17:29). It was a symbol of prosperity and having everything in plenty. That is why the Promised Land is described as "a land flowing with milk and honey" (Ex. 3:8, 17; Lev. 20:24; Num. 13:27; Deut. 6:3; Josh. 5:6; Jer. 11:5; Ezek. 20:6, 15). It was a symbol of the best and most satisfying sweetness. Therefore, a lover would compare his beloved with honey: "Your lips, my bride, drip honey; Honey and milk are under your tongue." (Song of Sol. 4:11; also 5:1).

For this very reason Solomon advised his son to eat honey (Prov. 24:13). However, he was not really speaking of the literal honey found in a forest. The next verse says, "Know that wisdom is thus for your soul." What Solomon was saying in these two verses is that if you have ever tasted honey from a comb, you will have some idea that just as the honey from a comb is sweet to your taste, wisdom is important for your soul. Just as honey is a delight to the taste and satisfies man's physical hunger, wisdom satisfies your soul. Just as you would look for the best food to satisfy your hunger, you would do well if you would strive to achieve wisdom to satisfy your soul.

And so the Scripture compares the Word of God—the source of true wisdom—with honey, even honey from the comb. David, who had tasted the Word of God, wrote from his own experience; "The judgments of the LORD are ... more desirable than gold, yes, than much fine gold; Sweeter also than honey and the drippings of the honeycomb" (Ps. 19:9–10). Also, "How sweet are Your words to my taste! Yes, sweeter than honey to my mouth!" (Ps. 119:103). When the prophet Ezekiel ate the scroll of the Word of God he said, "It was sweet as honey in my mouth" (Ezek. 3:3).

Actually, the Word of God is far more satisfying than honey, than anything else we can find under the sun. When we eat too much honey, we find that we loathe it; "A sated man loathes honey" (Prov. 27:7); and "Have you found honey? Eat only what you need, That you not have it in excess and vomit it" (Prov. 25:16). And so Solomon said, "It is not good to eat much honey" (Prov. 25:27). However, with the Word of God, the more you eat, the sweeter it gets; the more you devour it, the more you want it.

Also, honey nor anything else, nothing can compare with the satisfaction, joy, and fulfillment we receive from the Word of God. The blessings of the Word of God are from out of this world—literally! God does bless us with every good thing of this world to satisfy us (Ps. 104:28; 81:16). However, nothing can satisfy us like the Word of God, the fellowship and sweet communion with God through time in His Word. As David said, "O God, You are my God; I shall seek You earnestly; My soul thirsts for You, my flesh yearns for You, In a dry and weary land where there is no water." And he said, in God "my soul is satisfied as with marrow and fatness, and my mouth offers praises with joyful lips" (Ps. 63:1, 5).

The temptation is always there, even for us who would consider ourselves as mature disciples, to seek satisfaction in the things of the world; to consider ourselves "blessed" when God provides us with far more than just meeting our needs. We, too, need to respond to the invitation, "Why do you spend money for what is not bread, And your wages for what does not satisfy? Listen carefully to Me, and eat what is good, And delight yourself in abundance" (Isa. 55:2).

My prayer, and your prayer, like David's, should be, "O Lord ... deliver my soul ... from men of the world, whose portion is in this life; and whose belly Thou dost fill with Thy treasure; they are satisfied with children, and leave their abundance to their babes. As for me, I shall behold Thy face in righteousness; I will be satisfied with Thy likeness when I awake" (Ps. 17:13–15).

"Eat honey for it is good, yes, the honey from the comb is sweet to your taste" (Ps. 24:13). Because if you have tasted this honey, you would know how satisfying God's Word is to your soul.

Are you eating this honey? You can never have enough! That is the only thing that can really satisfy you.

> I'd rather have Jesus than silver or gold;
> I'd rather be His than riches untold.
> He's fairer than lilies of rarest bloom;
> He's sweeter than honey from out the comb.
>
> —Rhea F. Miller, 1922[1]

—Dr. Imanuel G. Christian

Missionary to his homeland of India and author of
several Bible commentaries in the Gujarati language of India

Preface

WHEN THE SONS of Israelites were in bondage in Egypt, they cried out to God for deliverance. The Lord saw their affliction and promised to deliver them from the hands of the Egyptians and take them to a land "flowing with milk and honey." He led them out of Egypt on a journey—a pilgrimage—to the Promised Land. Along the way, the sons of Israel would experience both victories and setbacks as they crossed three "thresholds" and several milestones in their relationship with the Lord. At each stage, the Lord revealed a new truth to them, which enabled them to continue to grow in their relationship with Him.

The Milk and Honey Man is a study and explanation of the Bible's message to these people of Moses' generation and to those of us in the twenty-first century. It reveals how believers in Moses' time became children of God and how we, likewise, can become a part of God's family today. The book also describes how believers of Moses' time made their commitment to serve God, and it encourages people of our time to do so as well. Furthermore, it explains how the sons of Israel experienced the abundant life of God and how we can also experience abundant life in Christ.

We learn in Romans 15:4, "For whatever was written in earlier times was written for our instruction, that through perseverance and the encouragement of the Scriptures we might have hope." As you explore this book and the accompanying diagrams, you will discover how what happened to the Israelites who followed Moses is a prophecy and a picture—a type—of the experience of the Christian. For Christians, this is a reward and a plan for life.

CHAPTER 1

Typology

How to Look for Milk and Honey

1 CORINTHIANS 10:1–11

You will make known to me the path of life; in Your presence is fullness of joy; in Your right hand there are pleasures forever.

—Ps. 16:11

WHAT IS THE path of life a person takes as he or she draws near to God? The Old Testament story of the Israelites' pilgrimage from Egypt to the Promised Land provides a pattern of the Christian's journey of faith. We were alerted to that in 1 Corinthians 10:1–11:

For I do not want you to be unaware, brethren, that our fathers were all under the cloud and all passed through the sea; and all were baptized into Moses in the cloud and in the sea; and all ate the same spiritual food; and all drank the same spiritual drink, for they were drinking from a spiritual rock which followed them; and the rock was Christ. Nevertheless, with most of them God was not well-pleased; for they were laid low in the wilderness. Now these things happened as examples for us, so that we would not crave evil things as they also craved. Do not be idolaters, as some of them were; as it was written, 'THE PEOPLE SAT DOWN TO EAT AND DRINK, AND STOOD UP TO PLAY.' Nor let us act immorally, as some of them did, and twenty-three thousand fell in one day. Nor let us try the Lord, as some of them did, and were destroyed by the serpents. Nor grumble, as some of them did, and were destroyed by the destroyer. Now these things happened to them as an example, and they were written for our instruction, upon whom the ends of the ages have come.

In Genesis 35:1, we read that God told Jacob, whom He later renamed Israel, to "arise, go up to Bethel and live there, and make an altar there to God, who appeared to you when you fled from your brother Esau." So Jacob and his twelve sons and their families settled in the land of Canaan. Later, the Lord sent Joseph to Egypt in advance of his brothers to help deliver them from a future famine in the region. Although Joseph was a slave when he first arrived in Egypt, God orchestrated the events in his life and ultimately put him in a position of authority in the land so he could aid his brothers and their families during the crisis. So the children of Israel travelled to Egypt, where they remained for 400 years.

But during this time, as the book of Exodus recounts, the Egyptians grew wary of the sons of Israel. The Israelites were fruitful and multiplied in the land, and the Egyptians were concerned that they would side with Egypt's enemies (see Ex. 1:9) and that they would lose their brick-making slaves. So, in time, the Israelites' life in Goshen actually became bondage, and they remained there until they were delivered by the Lord through His servant Moses, and, subsequently, were brought to and resettled in the Promised Land—the land of "milk and honey."

The sons of Israel had a promise from God regarding the destination He had planned for them—the final location where He intended for them to conduct their lives. They could anticipate freedom from bondage as they made their pilgrimage from Egypt to Canaan. The difficulties and challenges they faced are examples for us today as we pursue God's will in our situations. In observing their travels, we can better understand aspects of our own pilgrimage through life and the Lord's faithfulness to bring us to His destiny for us.

Types and Anti-types

Before we can begin to make this parallel between the Israelites' exodus from Egypt and the Christians' journey with God, we first need to examine a principle in interpreting Scripture known as "typology." Typology is the study of people, events, and principles in the Old Testament for the purpose of determining how they correlate to certain people, events, and truths in the New Testament. The typology we discover in the Old Testament is the key to fully understanding the lessons we learn in the New Testament about our pilgrimage to become a Milk and Honey Man.

Typology

A "type" is a person or thing in the Old Testament that foreshadows an "anti-type" (the fulfillment) in the New Testament. It is both a picture and a prediction of some future person, place, or event. Both are necessary; without a type, you cannot have an anti-type; and without an anti-type, you cannot have a type. In the original Greek, the word for "type" (also translated as "example") is *tupos,* which means a mark or impression caused by a blow or a stamp. It is a copy of the original. "... Adam, who is a *type* of Him [Jesus] who was to come" (Rom. 5:14).

The Lord Jesus often used the Old Testament typologically to illustrate various truths. In Matthew 16:4, when the Pharisees and Sadducees asked Jesus to show them a sign from heaven, He said, "An evil and adulterous generation seeks after a sign; and a sign will not be given it, except the sign of Jonah." In the Old Testament account, Jonah was swallowed by a great fish, was in its stomach for three days (see Jonah 1:17), and then was vomited onto dry land (see 2:10). Jonah represented a type of Jesus, who would spend three days in the tomb and then be resurrected from the dead.

It is always important to be cautious when attempting to determine the validity of a type. Sometimes, commentators will make extreme claims of a type when there is insufficient evidence to support the claim, and it is easy for a reader of the Bible to misinterpret the text, seeing a type where none exists. A type must always have an anti-type, and there must be a close parallel in meaning, particularly in major points. However, the two might not necessarily match on all points.

Generally, you can know that a type is valid if the New Testament identifies the fulfillment of that type by using the words "type" (see Rom. 5:14), "example" (see 1 Cor. 10:6), "allegory" (see Gal. 4:24), "shadow" (see Heb. 10:1) or "copy" (see Heb. 8:5). If the New Testament does not make use of one of these descriptive words, the type can still be considered valid if the text makes it clear that a certain person, event, or truth in the New Testament is being prefigured in the Old Testament. For example, in Luke 24:13–32, when Jesus spoke to the two men on the way to Emmaus, we read that "beginning with Moses and with all the prophets, He explained to them the things concerning Himself in all the Scriptures." Another example is found in 1 Corinthians 10:4, where Paul said, "the spiritual rock which followed them [the Israelites in the Exodus from Egypt] ... was Christ."

The story of Joseph is another illustration of a type. Joseph became his family's deliverer when he brought all seventy of his relatives to Egypt to protect them from a famine. Note, also, that the Bible does not record any sin against him. Of course, this does not mean that Joseph was sinless, but that his life was characterized by loyalty and service to God. Thus, Joseph is considered by some to be a type of Christ. The Lord Jesus Christ Himself was the anti-type, the fulfillment of the type; He had no sin and is our deliverer.

Look for these types and anti-types in your own study of the Bible. Such study will help you realize that even though a number of different people wrote the Bible, God is the one and only author. All Scripture fits together magnificently! We do well when we recognize that "no prophecy of Scripture is a matter of one's own interpretation, for no prophecy was ever made by an act of human will, but men moved by the Holy Spirit spoke from God" (2 Peter 1:20–21).

Natural, Carnal, Spiritual

In 1 Corinthians 10:1–10, Paul describes how Moses and the Israelites were under the cloud (v. 1), passed through the sea (v. 1), were baptized into Moses (v. 2), ate spiritual food (manna) (v. 3), drank from the spiritual rock that followed them (Christ) (v. 4), craved evil things (v. 6), were idolaters (v. 7), acted immorally (v. 8), tried the patience of the Lord (v. 9), and grumbled (v. 10). In verses 6 and 11, Paul uses the word *tupos* to show that these are types of some actions that we, too, have followed—but should not. When Joseph revealed his identity to his brothers, he was able to tell them that even though they meant their actions "for evil, God meant it for good." We, too, would do well to trust our "trials" to God.

In analyzing the Israelites' pilgrimage from Egypt to Canaan to determine how their journey represents a type in the spiritual journey of a Christian, it is important to be aware of the three fundamental conditions that represent all humans. These three conditions can be described as "the natural man," "the carnal man," and "the spiritual man." Let's look at each of these three conditions in more detail.

The Natural Man

Natural man is lost. As Paul writes, "A natural man does not accept the things of the Spirit of God, for they are foolishness to him; and cannot understand them, because they are spiritually appraised." The natural man cannot accept the things of God because he has not received the Lord Jesus Christ as his Savior. He is not born again, and thus he is spiritually dead.

The Carnal Man

Although the carnal man has God's Spirit, he still does many things through human effort, by his "flesh." Paul described this category of believers in 1 Corinthians 3:1–3 when he said, "And I, brethren, could not speak to you as spiritual men, but as to men of flesh, as to infants in Christ. I gave you milk to drink, not solid food; for you were not yet able to receive it. Indeed, even now you are not yet able, for you are still fleshly [worldly, carnal]. For since there is jealousy and strife among you, are you not fleshly and are you not walking like mere men?"

The writer of Hebrews also makes reference to this person in Hebrews 5:11–14: "For though by this time you ought to be teachers, you have need again for someone to teach you the elementary principles of the oracles of God, and you have come to need milk and not solid food."

The carnal man is a babe in Christ. He only drinks milk and does not take in spiritual meat as older children and adults do. There are two possible reasons for this: (1) because he has not been born again for very long, or (2) because he has failed to grow spiritually. In the second case, the level of maturity in a carnal Christian will be a matter of degrees. It can be affected by how frequently he reads the Bible, or by how frequently he attends corporate worship, or by how frequently he prays, or by how frequently he engages in Christian fellowship, or by the quantity and quality of his service to the Lord and the finances he gives to Christian work. It is also affected by the number of years the person has been engaging in all of those activities.

Make no mistake—one does not become a Christian by engaging in any of these activities. Furthermore, God does not love a person more because he practices them. There are no "brownie points" for doing a lot of service. A person cannot buy favor by making large contributions; rather, it is what comes from the heart of that person that indicates his spiritual maturity. If a person's heart is strongly committed to the Lord, it will show up in the works he does.

The Spiritual Man

Paul describes the spiritual man in 1 Corinthians 2:15–16: "But he who is spiritual appraises all things, yet he himself is to be appraised by no one. For who has known the mind of the Lord, that he will instruct Him? But we have the mind of Christ." Does the spiritual man ever sin? Yes! But he repents of it and seeks to live according to the Word of God. He tries to learn what the Scripture says, and then he seeks to obey it, tell it, share it, and reflect it. This is the goal for all Christians.

From the Natural Man to the Spiritual Man

When an individual is in the process of drawing near to God, he moves from the natural man to the carnal man to the spiritual man. This natural/carnal/spiritual (N-C-S) trip can be seen as a parallel to the Egypt/wilderness/Canaan (E-W-C) journey that the Israelites took during the Exodus. Dr. Charles Solomon, founder of Grace Fellowship International, makes a similar observation: "The journey of the children of Israel from Egypt into Canaan is a comparison for the stages of spiritual growth in the Christian."[2]

As we observe the journey of the sons of Israel from the land of bondage in Egypt to the land of milk and honey in Canaan, we are able to recognize the pattern for Christian growth as taught in the New Testament. By understanding the Egypt to Canaan story as a "type," we can then begin to comprehend the journey of a person from a natural man to a spiritual man (N-C-S) and evaluate our own journey to see where we are in the pilgrimage.

Map of the Pilgrimage

The following diagram is the first chronological "map" that compares the physical journey of the sons of Israel to those taking the pilgrimage of the Christian life in the twenty-first century (the anti-type in the New Testament). The Old Testament locations of Egypt, the wilderness, and Canaan are spiritual types of which the Natural Man, the Carnal Man and the Spiritual Man are the fulfillment.

TYPOLOGY
CHRONOLOGICAL MAP OF THE PILGRIMAGE

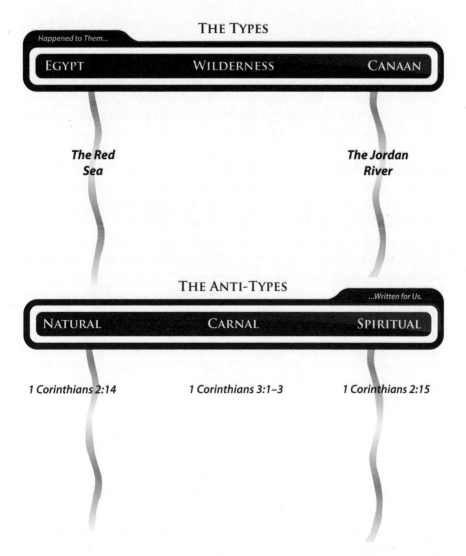

THE TYPES

Happened to Them...

| EGYPT | WILDERNESS | CANAAN |

The Red
Sea

The Jordan
River

THE ANTI-TYPES

...Written for Us.

| NATURAL | CARNAL | SPIRITUAL |

1 Corinthians 2:14   1 Corinthians 3:1–3   1 Corinthians 2:15

Notice in the above map that the Israelites were moving from bondage in Egypt (the natural man) to freedom in "the land of milk and honey" (the spiritual man), where they would "set up shop" to represent the Lord.

The Land of Milk and Honey

The first use of the term "the land of milk and honey" to describe the Promised Land is found in Exodus 3:7–8 and comes as a promise from God. "The LORD said, 'I have surely seen the affliction of My people who are in Egypt, and have given heed to their cry because of their taskmasters, for I am aware of their sufferings. So I have come down to deliver them from the power of the Egyptians, and to bring them up from that land to a good and spacious land, to a land flowing with milk and honey.'"

Milk was part of the diet of the Hebrews from patriarchal times, and, where there was abundance of milk, it was possible for them to enjoy the added delicacy of cream or curdled milk (Isa. 7:22). Hence we see the attraction of the land of Canaan as a land flowing with milk and honey, for the rich supply of milk was an indication of the pasturage available.[3] Honey was also readily available in Galilee—a fact that was well known by those in the region.[4] Thus, "the land of milk and honey" portrays a fertile land that supplies rich pasturage for cattle, enabling them to give such abundant milk that the land is said to flow with it, and produces many kinds of flowers, which provide food for honey-producing bees.[5]

The Promised Land offered prosperity, abundance, and blessings from God. The fact that Dathan and Abiram, two embittered Israelites wandering in the wilderness who took part in Korah's rebellion (Num. 16:13), described Egypt as the "land of milk and honey" is a clear indication that the term was used to describe what was perceived to be a desirable place to live.[6] As we will see below, it was also a place that offered rest. All of these blessings are indicative of the inheritance that the sons of Israel would receive in Canaan, which is symbolic of what the spiritual man will receive.

In Exodus 19:5–6, God told the Israelites, "Now then, if you will indeed obey My voice and keep My covenant, then you shall be My own possession among all the peoples, for the earth is Mine; and you shall be to Me a kingdom of priests [to the world of their day] and a holy nation." It was all about the Lord! It was all about serving Him. This was not about the Israelites having an easy life or about them having fun along the way. Yes, life would be more pleasurable and easier for them when they were in His land, but He wanted them to know that they were there for a reason. They were there to serve Him. They were there to glorify and honor Him.

Using Accurate Types to Interpret Scripture

Some people believe and teach that the Promised Land is a type of heaven. The rationale seems to be that the Israelites had reached their final destiny and it was a great place, which could obviously be said about heaven. However, as we discussed previously, it is important to be cautious when attempting to determine the identity of a type in the Old Testament. In this case, there are four main reasons why the Promised Land could not represent a type for heaven.

First, it is important to remember that there was sin in the Promised Land. For example, in Joshua 6:17–18, the Lord warned the sons of Israel before they attacked Jericho, "The city shall be under the ban, it and all that is in it belongs to the LORD ... but as for you, only keep yourselves from the things under the ban, so that you do not covet them and take some of the things under the ban, and make the camp of Israel accursed and bring trouble on it."

However, as we read in Joshua 7:1, "The sons of Israel acted unfaithfully in regard to the things under the ban, for Achan ... from the tribe of Judah, took some of the things under the ban, therefore the anger of the LORD burned against the sons of Israel." Subsequently, the Israelites attempted to conquer the town of Ai and failed, resulting in thirty-six of their own being killed. Joshua prayed to the Lord about the matter, and the Lord said to him,

> Rise up! Why is it that you have fallen on your face? Israel has sinned, and they have also transgressed My covenant which I commanded them. And they have even taken some of the things under the ban and have both stolen and deceived. Moreover, they have also put them among their own things. Therefore the sons of Israel cannot stand before their enemies; they turn their backs before their enemies, for they have become accursed. I will not be with you anymore unless you destroy the things under the ban from your midst.
>
> —Josh. 7:10–12

From this, we observe the following:

> There was sin in the Promised Land. There is no sin in heaven. This does not match and therefore is not a type.

A second reason why the Promised Land could not represent a type for heaven is because the sons of Israel had war in the land. When they entered the Promised Land, at the Lord's instruction, the sons of Israel fought against various enemies and progressively took over parts of the land. These were areas in which the twelve tribes would establish residence. The battles were physical battles, with people being killed.

Although Scripture states there will be war in heaven between Satan and angels in which Satan will be cast out (Rev. 12:7–9), this is not the anti-type for the war in the Promised Land. Arrival in the Promised Land is not a type of arrival in heaven. Thus we can determine the following:

> There was war by the people in the Promised Land. There is no war by God's people in heaven. This does not match and therefore is not a type.

Third, the requirements of the Mosaic covenant included responsibilities of those who would occupy the Promised Land. These responsibilities included being a kingdom of priests. The sons of Israel had the priestly responsibility in connection with the non-Israelites they encountered. From this we can determine:

> The people of God in the Promised Land had priestly responsibilities. There are no priestly responsibilities for the people of God in heaven. This does not match and therefore is not a type.

A final observation is that if the Promised Land represents a type of heaven, it would mean that Moses is spending eternity in another place, as the Lord prohibited him from entering the Promised Land.

A Place of Rest

Based on these four reasons, I believe that the Promised Land is not a type of heaven, and because of this, I believe that many people have misinterpreted portions of the book of Hebrews. For instance, in Hebrews 3:7–19, the writer states that the Israelites were not able to enter the Promised Land because of their unbelief. The text does *not* say that they were unable to enter because they were unbelievers; it just states that they had an unbelieving heart (v. 10). The Israelites were not unbelievers—they were redeemed people (Ex. 15:13)—but they had an untrusting heart. They were not willing to trust the Lord to bring them into Canaan.

The Israelites were supposed to enter the Promised Land. In Hebrews (3:11, 18; 4:3, 5, 8–11), the writer refers to it as "My [God's] rest" or just "rest." This refers back to the seventh day of creation, when God rested from His works. This helps to clarify what this place of "rest" was for the sons of Israel: "it was the territory where they would accomplish God's will without working." They would live by faith, not works. They would not work; the Lord would. Likewise, when we enter into the Lord's rest, we enter a place or circumstance that allows, enables, and even demands that we rest from our works (self-effort).

Moving Toward Milk and Honey

Pursuing milk and honey can be enhanced by studying the types from Egypt to Canaan. Now let's see who the Milk and Honey Man is.

Is it you?

CHAPTER 2

Slaves in Egypt

Bondage in the Life of the Milk and Honey Man

Exodus 1–3

THE ISRAELITES' JOURNEY from Egypt to Canaan reveals how God faithfully supervised, provided for, and tested the obedience of the sons of Israel. However, before we begin our study of the journey, we first need to look at the initial problem that prompted them to leave Egypt: bondage.

The Lord had promised His servant Abram (later called "Abraham") that he would have many descendants (Gen. 12:2). Despite the fact that Abram was old and had no children, he believed that God would fulfill this promise. His belief was reckoned to him as righteousness (Gen. 15:6), and he became "the father of all who believe" (Rom. 4:11). The Lord also promised to give the land of Canaan to Abram's descendants. At this point, Abram asked for a guarantee.

In response to Abram's request, the Lord used a practice common in the ancient Near East at the time to ratify the promise. In this ceremony, two animals were cut in half, and then the two parties who were making the contract (the agreement or the covenant) walked between the cut pieces (Gen. 15:10–21). This was somewhat like two parties shaking hands on a deal they made. By doing this, the Lord was assuring Abram of the possession of the land.

After Abram had collected the animals for the ceremony, he fell into a deep sleep. While he slept, the Lord told him of the bondage that his descendants would one day endure in Egypt: "Know for certain that your descendants will be strangers in a land that is not theirs, where they will be enslaved and oppressed four hundred years. But I will also judge the nation whom they will serve, and afterward they will come out with many possessions" (Gen. 15:13–14).

Then the Lord, represented by "a smoking oven and a flaming torch" (Gen. 15:17), passed between the two pieces. Because Abram was asleep, he did not take part in his portion of the ceremony. The covenant with Abram depended totally on the Lord Himself to fulfill it. It was a one-sided covenant. Unilateral! There were no requirements for Abram to perform. There was nothing for him to do, but believe.

The Experience of Bondage

Years later, Abraham's great-grandson Joseph was sold to Ishmaelite tradesmen by his brothers. Thus, Joseph was the first of the Israelites to be placed in bondage to the Egyptians. However, the Lord gave Joseph divine success while he was in Egypt, and eventually he was called upon to interpret the Pharaoh's dreams. The dreams that Joseph interpreted revealed that a famine was coming to the land, and the Pharaoh was so impressed with Joseph's wisdom that he placed him in charge of the whole land of Egypt (Gen. 41:1–45).

Joseph began to stockpile grain during the next seven years of plenty so that when the famine came, the Egyptians would have enough food to survive. Through his actions, and by virtue of his position, he was able to become the deliverer for his entire family. He moved his father, eleven brothers, and their families to Goshen in Egypt, and Pharaoh granted them favor because of all that Joseph was doing for Egypt. The sons of Israel were shepherds. The Egyptians did not like sheep, so the two groups kept separate. There was no intermarriage; however, the Israelites did multiply rapidly. In this way, God developed a people of His own, a nation (the Israelites) within a nation (Egypt). These were the chosen people.

Life for the Israelites wasn't overly difficult while Joseph was alive, and even after Joseph and the Pharaoh died, there was initially no great calamity between the sons of Israel and the Egyptians because of the high regard with which Joseph was held. However, as time passed, the Egyptians forgot about Joseph. The Israelites had multiplied so greatly by this time that their numbers had become a threat to the Egyptians, and it was at this point that the Egyptians resorted to slavery to keep the people under their control. Note the progression of the relationship between the Egyptians and the sons of Israel: "Glad to have you here"—"Not sure who you are"—"You are a threat, and therefore we must dominate you."

It is said that if you place a frog in a kettle of boiling water, it will immediately jump out. However, if you place the frog in a kettle of water at room temperature and then gradually heat up the kettle on a stove, the frog will adjust to the ever-increasing temperature and just sit there until it is eventually overcome with heat and dies. This was similar to the experience of the Israelites. Their servitude increased progressively over time until it became unbearable.

Bondage and slavery were a fact of life for the Israelites. The Egyptians "appointed taskmasters over them to afflict them with hard labor" (Ex. 1:11). They "made their lives bitter with hard labor in mortar and bricks and at all kinds of labor in the field, all their labors which they rigorously imposed on them" (Ex. 1:14). The Israelites did not want to be in bondage. They were unhappy, but they saw no other option! The sons of Israel could not get themselves out of bondage, and they did not know how they could be delivered from bondage. So they "groaned because of their slavery and cried out [to God] for help" (Ex. 2:23 ESV).

God knew how to get His people out of bondage, and He "heard their groaning and remembered His covenant with Abraham, Isaac, and Jacob. God saw the sons of Israel, and God took notice of them" (Ex. 2:24–25). When the Egyptians gave the Israelites hard labor and even resorted to killing the male babies to reduce the population, He spared the life of Moses and even orchestrated events so that he would grow up in Pharaoh's royal household. Moses' fellow Israelites, however, were born into bondage. They were under cruel taskmasters until God delivered them.

The story of how God delivered the sons of Israel from Egypt is one that is told over and over again. They remembered how the bondage was bitter, fruitless, and repugnant and how wonderful and powerful God was in bringing about their deliverance, redemption, and salvation. For instance, Joshua was one of the sons of Israel who was forced to make bricks under the demands of Egyptian taskmasters. He saw the ten plagues in Egypt, spied out the Promised Land, wandered in the wilderness forty years, and then led them across the Jordan River and into the Promised Land. At the end of his life, he gave a summary message in which he said, "The LORD our God is He who brought us up out of the land of Egypt, from the house of bondage" (Josh. 24:17).

The telling of the story of deliverance is also a model for Christians to use to tell their personal testimony of salvation over and over again. Such was the case with the apostle Paul after he was struck blind on the road to

Damascus in Acts 9:1–19. When he regained his sight and experienced salvation, he gave his testimony in Acts 22:2–21 and 26:1–23.

The Bondage of Sin

The bondage of the sons of Israel in Egypt is a symbol (or type) of our bondage to sin. The Israelites were held in bondage, and their story was written so that we could learn about our own bondage to sin. Consider these concepts:

1. Adam and Eve sinned in the garden of Eden (Gen. 3), and Adam's sin was passed on to all who were linked to him by physical birth. This means that by our natural birth—that is, our physical birth—we come into the world in the condition of sin.

2. Jesus Christ, the Righteous One, was *not* linked to the blood of Adam by physical birth,[7] nor did He commit any sin of His own. As such, He was/is the head of a race of righteous ones. Believers in the sacrifice and resurrection of the Lord Jesus Christ are born again into newness of life (in other places in Scripture believers in Christ are described as being "adopted" into the family of God; see Rom. 8:15, 23; 9:4; Gal. 4:5; Eph. 1:5). Thus, those who have not received Christ are still in their sin. They are still unsaved.

3. Bondage is a fact for non-Christians and was a fact for believers prior to their salvation. Jesus said, "Truly, truly, I say to you, everyone who commits sin is the slave of sin" (John 8:34). The apostle Paul referred to the Christians in Rome as those "who were slaves of sin" (Rom. 6:17) and said, "Knowing this, that our old self was crucified with Him, in order that our body of sin might be done away with, so that we would no longer be slaves to sin; for he who has died is freed from sin" (Rom. 6:6–7). To the Christians in Galatia, he wrote, "Do not be subject again to a yoke of slavery" (Gal. 5:1).

4. Initially, the Israelites did not resent their bondage. Similarly, because of the freedoms people have in America, many who are brought up here do not know that they are in bondage. People who are brought up in a society of relative freedom often do not realize their enslavement, nor do they consider themselves to be in bondage. Many Americans are brought up in an environment where drugs, alcohol, smoking, bitterness, hatred, prejudice, greed, and gluttony are prevalent. They are enslaved to their bodily/soulish pursuits.

15

5. It seems that those who are in bondage gradually come to recognize this fact. They did not ever want to be in bondage, and they want to be free from it! Many non-Christians are miserable in their bondage.

6. The Israelites did not perceive that they had another option available to them other than their bondage, just as non-Christians today do not realize that they have another option available to them other than being trapped in a state of sin. Romans 14:23 says, "whatever is not from faith [in Jesus Christ] is sin."

7. The sons of Israel did not know how to get out of bondage, and non-Christians today do not know how to be released from their bondage to sin. They do not know how to overcome their unbelief and need those of us who have experienced God's salvation to tell them how to be free. Paul says that God "gave us the ministry of reconciliation" (2 Cor. 5:18). Jesus instructed us, "Go ... and make disciples of all the nations" (Matt. 28:19).

8. If it gets bad enough, some non-Christians will call upon God for deliverance, just as the Hebrews did 3,400 years ago (and as those of us who are now Christians did in our lives).

Bondage in America today is a little different than it was in ancient times. The slave masters are not so easily recognized, but they still exist. Drug addicts know bondage, confessed alcoholics understand bondage, members of Overeaters Anonymous believe there is bondage, and chain smokers experience bondage. Some people are in bondage to bitterness, while others are in bondage to lust, bad language, lewdness ... the list goes on and on. Like the sons of Israel, we are unable to free ourselves from the bondage of sin.

However, for those who cry out to God, He will bring someone (or something—the Bible, a tract, a book) to show the way to deliverance. "For the eyes of the LORD move to and fro throughout the earth that He may strongly support those whose heart is completely His" (2 Chron. 16:9). The bondage of the Israelites is a type of our bondage to sin prior to our salvation. "Milk and honey" was to be found in the Promised Land—not in Egypt.

Definitions and Descriptions of Sin

There are many Hebrew and Greek words that refer to the concept of sin, but basically it means "missing the mark," with the "mark" being God's standard of holiness and righteousness. This implies not only missing the correct target but also hitting the *wrong* target. Sin is always contrary to the holiness of God. It is described in terms such as "iniquity," "wickedness," "ungodliness," "unrighteousness," and "lawlessness."

Deeds of Sin

The plural "sins" refers to attitudes held, thoughts conceived, words spoken, and deeds done that are contrary to God's design for holiness and righteousness. The word can be used in the singular, but it still refers to these things. This also is called the "deeds of the flesh" (Gal. 5:19).[8]

The First Human Sin

Adam was told, "From the Tree of the Knowledge of Good and Evil you shall not eat, for in the day that you eat from it you will surely die" (Gen. 2:17). When he disobeyed God and ate from the tree anyway, he was separated from God and died spiritually. Proof of Adam's separation from God was that he recognized his nakedness and subsequently made a loin covering of fig leaves. He also hid from God, because he knew he was guilty.

The covering of fig leaves was Adam and Eve's solution to their problem. It was "self-effort." But God had a different solution: "The Lord God made garments of skin for Adam and his wife, and clothed them" (Gen. 2:21). God used the skin of an animal to make their garments, which meant that an animal had to give its life so they could have clothes. Adam was forgiven of his sin because of the shedding of blood by a substitute. Adam accepted God's solution by wearing the skin of the animal, and in this way he was forgiven.

Inherited Sin

Adam's sin was passed on to all who were linked to him by physical birth. Adam is the "head" of a race of sinners (Rom. 5:12, 14), and because of this, everyone who comes into the world does so in the condition of sin. As Paul writes, "All have sinned and fall short of the glory of God" (Rom. 3:23). This means that by our natural birth—that is, our physical birth—we come into the world in the condition of sin. This sin is within us, and it includes the ability to commit acts or deeds of sin as well as the motivation to do so. We come into the world guilty, and a penalty is due because of our condition.

Indwelling Sin

In Romans 6:6, Paul said that for those who have put their faith in Jesus Christ, "the old man" or "the old self" has been crucified with Christ. The sin was dealt with at the cross, and believers in Jesus Christ have been delivered from the power of inherited sin. However, Christians still have the ability and even the motivation to commit sin. In Romans 7, Paul said he struggled with what he called the "sin that dwells in me" (v. 17 and v. 20) and the "sin which is in my members" (v. 23).

Sin Nature

Although the term "sin nature" has widespread use in Christian circles, it does not appear in Scripture. It is sometimes used to describe what I refer to as "inherited sin," sometimes to describe "indwelling sin," and sometimes it is used to describe both concepts together as one. This last point—one term for two concepts—presents a problem. Inherited sin and indwelling sin are different.

The primary difference is that inherited sin involves bondage. The non-Christian is unable to do anything except sin because he or she is bound to it. But, as we saw in Romans 6:6–7, those who are crucified with Christ are now "freed from sin." They are no longer bound to it because they have been delivered from its power.

This important difference reveals that two things happened at the cross. First, as is commonly recognized, Jesus died for the sins of mankind as a substitute, and those who receive Him are forgiven. A second point that is often overlooked, however, is that Jesus died to sin, thus breaking its power. Therefore, for believers in Christ, "our old self was crucified with Him, in order that our body of sin might be done away with, so that we would no longer be slaves to sin" (Rom. 6:6). This is what distinguishes inherited sin from indwelling sin.

Another way to explain the distinction is by using the Latin terms that describe the capability or inability to commit sin. *Non posse non peccare*, "not able to not sin," represents a person who is in bondage to inherited sin. *Posse peccare posse non peccare*, "able to sin and able to not sin," represents a person who has indwelling sin and has the capabilities of either sinning or not sinning.

As we stated, a non-Christian cannot not sin. Or, said another way, the only thing a non-Christian can do is sin because "whatever is not from faith is sin" (Rom. 14:23). If faith in Jesus Christ is required to conduct life and a non-Christian, by definition, does not have faith in Jesus Christ, then there is nothing that person can do that does not fall into the category of sin.

Sinners and Saints

It is worthwhile here to note that there are two categories of people: sinners and saints. Sinners are those whose only option is to commit sins. Note that they might do things that seem to be good, but "whatever is not from faith is sin" still applies. Saints (literally "holy ones" in the original Greek) are those who have received Jesus Christ and, thus, His righteousness. All who are born again are saints due to Jesus' righteousness, not their own. Granted, some saints might act like sinners, but that is not the basis of the meaning of the word. Saints who sin do not become sinners, but sinning saints! They are no longer sinners, but saints who sometimes sin.

Also, note that being tempted to sin does not constitute committing a sin. Yielding to the temptation is an act of sin, but temptation itself is not sin.

The Make-up of Humans

In order to better comprehend how inherited sin and indwelling sin work in each of us, it might be helpful at this point to discuss the three differing views on how humans were created. Some believe that humans have a dichotomous makeup; some believe that humans have a trichotomous make up; and some believe that humans have a monochotomous make up.

Many people believe that humans are made up of two parts: material and immaterial. It is certainly true that we have a body, the part one can cut with a knife, and that we also have an immaterial part, which cannot be seen nor cut with a knife. This is referred to as the dichotomous view of how we are made.

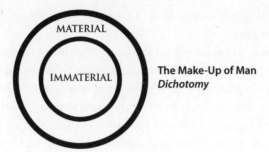

The Make-Up of Man
Dichotomy

Others argue that man is made up of three parts: body, soul, and spirit. The concept is found in 1 Thessalonians 5:23: "Now may the God of peace Himself sanctify you entirely; and may your spirit and soul and body be preserved complete, without blame at the coming of our Lord Jesus Christ." Hebrews 4:12 is also a supporting verse: "The word of God is living and active and sharper than any two-edged sword, and piercing as far as the division of soul and of spirit, both of joints and marrow, and able to judge the thoughts and intentions of the heart." This is referred to as the trichotomous view of how we are made.

The Make-Up of Man
Trichotomy

Finally, there are others who contend that man is a whole person, not to be divided into parts. This is referred to as the monochotomous view of how we are made.

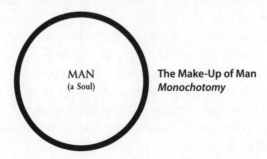

The Make-Up of Man
Monochotomy

Consider the following illustration. The mind, will, and emotions are found in the soul. A flower has a body, but no soul or spirit. As it grows in a field on a hot sunny day, it might wilt from the heat, but, having no soul, it cannot think (mind), "Wow, it surely is hot today," or, "I'm burning up; I would like (will) to go stand in the shade." The flower has a body, but no soul, and therefore no mind with which it can reason.

A dog has a body and soul. On that hot sunny day, the dog thinks (mind), "It sure is hot today. I'm going to go (will) stand in the shade." And he does! But a dog does not have a spirit. If a man goes over and kicks the dog, in his mind he will think, "That guy in the red shirt kicked me," his emotions will tell him, "I'm angry about it," and he will exercise his will when he turns to bite the man. But, having no spirit, the dog cannot conceive in his brain, "It was immoral for that guy to kick me."

All Three Concepts

The Greek word for soul is *psuche*. It is translated several ways in the New Testament and is used of the whole person (supporting the monochotomous view), of the immaterial part of man (supporting the dichotomous view), and of the third part of man (supporting the trichotomous view).[9] The uses of the term to describe the third part of man (the trichotomous view) can help us understand and pinpoint the concept of inherited sin in a man.

The Make-Up of Man Before Salvation

The Spirit is Dead

In Paul's letter to the Ephesians, he wrote, "You were dead in your trespasses and sins" (Eph. 2:1). Were the bodies of the Ephesians dead? No! The Ephesian believers were alive, and he expected them to read his letter. Was their soul—their mind, emotions, and/or will—dead? No! The Ephesians could still think, and Paul expected them to understand his letter. So, to what was Paul referring when he said they were dead in their trespasses? Paul was referring to their spirit. Formerly, they had been spiritually dead.

Their inner being, which he called "the old man," had been dead. This was the location of inherited sin.

Thus, the Bible use *psuche* (soul) in various ways, but it is the trichotomous view that enables us to understand what part of man was dead and is now alive. Understanding that concept can help us move forward toward a victorious life.

Moving Toward Milk and Honey

All of us have an ability and motivation to sin because we came into the world with sin as our master. The future Milk and Honey Man was born into bondage to inherited sin and must be delivered from it. The first step in being delivered from our sin is to become aware of it. Gaining that awareness is the starting place for deliverance from it and represents a milestone in our lives.

CHAPTER 3

The Ten Plagues in Egypt
The All-Powerful God of the Milk and Honey Man
Exodus 7:14–12:36

DELIVERANCE FOR THE sons of Israel could only come from God. Before that could happen, however, the Israelites had to learn Who God was and how powerful He was. Seeing His power at work in their situation could facilitate their willingness to trust Him and to follow Him in leaving the bondage in Egypt. God demonstrated His power to them through a series of dramatic plagues He inflicted on the Egyptians.

The Egyptians worshiped the gods of their mythology and looked to each of these gods for some specific benefit or deliverance. These idols, which were often made of wood, stone, or metal, represented an area of life man was trying to handle on his own apart from the one true God. God considered worship of these idols or false gods a sin, and the Egyptians' erroneous worship led to their judgment.[10] This judgment came in the form of the plagues.

The plagues from the true God were real plagues. They were judgments on the false gods of Egypt, and thus on the Egyptians who worshiped them. The plagues revealed the superiority of the one true God over each of the Egyptian false gods, and the complete victory that the plagues brought in freeing the sons of Israel from bondage proves that the Lord is Lord over everything. It is akin to the Israelites watching Elijah confront the prophets of Baal and their false god. After God won the contest, the people said, "The LORD, He is God; the LORD, He is God" (1 Kings 18:39). In this chapter, we will look at the nature of each of these plagues in greater detail to see how each represented a specific victory over a false Egyptian god.

Plague 1: The Nile Turned into Blood
Exodus 7:14–25

The Nile River is one of the greatest rivers of the world. In reference to its primary stream, it is also the longest river in the world, covering 4,160 miles.[11] In ancient times, it was the source of Egypt's livelihood. The floods that occurred each year in July and August made it possible for the Egyptians to grow the bountiful crops that were vital to their agriculture and economy.

Several facts about this situation can help us understand what was going on. The Egyptians considered Hapi to be the god of the Nile. In ancient Egyptian art, Hapi was portrayed as a man with women's breasts and a protruding belly.[12] This was supposed to indicate the god's fertility and, thus, his ability to nourish the land through the Nile's annual floods. The Egyptians did not know how or why the Nile flooded each year, but they believed that Hapi was in charge of the waters. They referred to the annual floods as the "arrival of Hapi" and worshiped him for the bountiful crops they believed he provided.

When Moses and Aaron first went to Pharaoh to secure the release of the sons of Israel, they said, "Thus says the LORD [YHWH], the God of Israel, 'Let My people go that they may celebrate a feast to Me in the wilderness'" (Ex. 5:1). But Pharaoh answered, "Who is the LORD that I should obey His voice to let Israel go? I do not know the LORD, and besides, I will not let Israel go" (Ex. 5:2). When a person questions who the Lord is, He is sure to show up. In Pharaoh's case, He was just about to reveal Himself in a powerful way and demonstrate that He was greater than the Egyptians' precious Nile River.

It is possible that when Moses later went to see the Pharaoh at the Nile River (Ex. 7:15), the Pharaoh was there to worship Hapi. John MacArthur notes that "Pharaoh habitually went to the river" and that "hymns of thanksgiving were often sung for the blessings brought by the Nile, the country's greatest, single economic resource."[13] Apparently, the Egyptians were giving thanks to some perceived authority higher than the Pharaoh, though it was merely a false god of their own imagination. When Moses met Pharaoh, he said to him, "Thus says the Lord, 'By this you shall know that I am the LORD: behold, I will strike the water that is in the Nile, with the staff that is in my hand, and it will be turned to blood'" (Ex. 7:17).

After Moses said this, Aaron raised his staff and struck the water of the Nile, and all the water was changed into blood (Ex. 7:20). In this way, the Lord proved that He was superior to Hapi, to the Nile River, and to the Egyptian's desire to control agriculture apart from dependence on the one true God. Proof of this plague's devastating effect was that the fish died (Ex. 7:21) and the Egyptians had to dig in the ground to get drinking water (Ex. 7:24).

God is God! It's a profound statement, and yet many don't believe it. He is more powerful than man, and more powerful than nature. He created both. Unlike false gods, which the Bible describes as "the work of man's hands, wood and stone, which neither see, nor hear, nor eat, nor smell" (Deut. 4:28), God is alive and at work in people's lives. Through this first plague, He proved to the Egyptians that He was more powerful than the inventions of men's minds. The Lord is God, and He was simply not willing to take second place to some false concept in the Egyptians' minds.

What false gods have you set up in your life? Is there any area in which you declare, "Hands off, God, I will make the decision on this one," or, "I can take care of this one myself"? If so, you have a false god in your life. God instructed Moses to bring His people out of the place of bondage (Ex. 3:1–10), and He wants to bring you out of bondage to that false god as well.

Plague 2: Frogs
Exodus 8:1–15

The annual inundation of the Nile, which brought fertility to the otherwise barren lands, also brought with it an inundation of frogs. Because these multitudes of frogs were born after the annual floods, they became a symbol of life and fertility to the Egyptians. The Egyptians worshiped the frogs and placed a ban on killing them in the land. Heqet was the name of the false god who represented the frogs and in the minds of the Egyptians, Heqet was a woman with a frog's head. Heqet was, in their minds, a goddess of birth and fertility, but the specific belief was that the breath of life came from her nostrils.

For the second plague, the Lord made this false god become a curse to the Egyptians. It was almost as if He were saying, "You like frogs? I'll give you frogs. I'll give you lots of them!" And He did. They were all over the land—in their houses, in their bedrooms (Ps. 105:30), in their courtyards, in their fields, everywhere.

God put into the hearts of husbands and wives the desire to have children when He commanded them to, "Be fruitful and multiply, and fill the earth, and subdue it" (Gen. 1:28). However, many in our current generation have attempted to supersede God's sovereign control over reproduction by setting up false gods of fertility. Some people, not wanting children, ignore God's command, while others take the opposite approach and try to find a human solution to barrenness, just as Abraham did when he tried to produce a child through his wife's maid, Hagar (Gen. 16:1–4).

Where do you find yourself on this spectrum? How would this particular plaque speak to your situation?

Plague 3: Gnats
Exodus 8:16–19

For the third plague, God had Moses strike the dust of the ground, and all the dust in Egypt became gnats. There is no doubt that this was one of the ten plagues, but which of the false gods did it represent? Even if there were no formal false god, it follows that there should be an object, practice, or characteristic that the Egyptians were elevating to a point of worship that God wanted to overturn.

In this case, it seems that the plague of gnats "may have been directed against the Egyptian priesthood. The priests prided themselves in their purity with their frequent washings and shavings."[14] Thus, the Lord polluted the prideful priests with the pesky insects. The King James Version translates this word "gnats" as "lice." Many people in America today are horrified that someone might discover their children have lice. Is that a pride problem? Dust was the origin.

Have you ever thought of yourself as prideful about cleanliness? Do you ever look with disdain at other people in society who live in filth and have no apparent embarrassment about it? Do you think that you are superior because of your cleanliness? Watch out for the gnats.

It's interesting to note that while Pharaoh's magicians were able to duplicate the first two plagues, they were not able to duplicate this one. When the gnats infested the land, they were forced to acknowledge, "This is the finger of God" (Ex. 8:19).

Plague 4: Flies
Exodus 8:20–32

For the fourth plague, God brought dense swarms of flies to the land of Egypt. These may have been dog flies, which fasten themselves to the human body, especially the eyelids.[15] Or they may have been ichneumon flies, which depicted the god Uatchit.[16] Another possibility is that they were of the species *stomoxys calcitrans*, which infests houses and stables, biting both men and animals. They are the principal transmitter of skin anthrax.[17]

Scholars are not united in their assessment of what type of specific flies were involved in the fourth plague, nor of the specific false god of Egypt which they represent. However, in Psalm 78:45, the psalmist, recounting the plagues in Egypt, relates that the swarms of flies "devoured" the Egyptians. Presumably, the false god was expected to protect the Egyptians from the flies, and the true God revealed His superiority to the false god by passing judgment on the Egyptians and making the plague happen.

In America today, we have screens on the doors and windows of our houses to prohibit a major invasion of flies. If we were to worship those screens, it might be similar to the Egyptians' worship of a false god. It seems to me that our culture is not presently subject to a parallel false god—for which we should be very thankful.

It is interesting to note that this was the first plague that did not affect the sons of Israel. In Exodus 8:22, God says, "But on that day I will set apart the land of Goshen, where My people are living, so that no swarms of flies will be there." It seems that a lesson the Lord was teaching His people was that they were to be distinct from the Egyptians. In addition, none of the remaining plagues applied to them.

Plague 5: Disease on Beasts
Exodus 9:1–7

After the plague of flies, the Lord instructed Moses, "Go to Pharaoh and speak to him, 'Thus says the LORD, the God of the Hebrews, "Let My people go, that they may serve Me. For if you refuse to let them go and continue to hold them, behold, the hand of the LORD will come with a very severe pestilence on your livestock which are in the field, on the horses, on the donkeys, on the camels, on the herds, and on the flocks"'" (Ex. 9:1–3).

This fifth plague involved a severe disease (possibly anthrax) on the Egyptians' livestock in the field. These animals were beasts of burden used in agriculture, transportation, and construction, and their death would have represented a negative effect on the economy of the Egyptians. The false god involved here may have been Hathor, an ancient goddess who was worshiped as a cow deity. According to some scholars, in Egyptian mythology, "Hathor [Egyptian for house of Horus] was originally a personification of the milky way, which was seen as the milk that flowed from the udders of a heavenly cow."[18]

As with the fourth plague, this plague on the livestock affected only the Egyptians; the animals of the sons of Israel did not get this disease. When the Lord told Moses to warn Pharaoh about this coming plague, He said He would make a distinction between the livestock of Israel and the livestock of Egypt. This, in effect, represented a distinction between the Hebrew God and the false gods of Egypt. To God, an Egyptian must have no part in a believer in Jehovah, and a believer in Jehovah must have no part in Egypt. As we learn in the New Testament, "Do not love the world nor the things in the world" (1 John 2:15).

When Pharaoh discovered that the sons of Israel were not affected by the plague, he sent someone to investigate the circumstances in Goshen. The men discovered that not even one of the Israelites' animals had died. But, nevertheless, "the heart of Pharaoh was hardened, and he did not let the people go" (Ex. 9:7).

Plague 6: Boils on Man and Beasts
Exodus 9:8–12

The sixth plague was an attack against the Egyptians' health. The Lord arranged for Moses to throw soot up into the air, which had the effect of producing boils and sores on both man and animals. The ashes came from one of the furnaces the Hebrews used to produce the bricks the Egyptians demanded from them.

In this instance, God attacked the false god, Sekhmet, who was thought to be the protector of human health. Sekhmet was seen, among other things, as a bearer of disease as well as the provider of cures to such ills. In fact, in antiquity the name "Sekhmet" literally became synonymous with physicians and surgeons. Many members of Sekhmet's priesthood were often considered to be equivalent to physicians.[19]

Once again, the Egyptian god was not up to the challenge. Moses threw the soot "toward the sky, and it became boils breaking out with sores on man and beast" (Ex. 9:10). Pharaoh's magicians were still hanging around. They, too, got struck with boils. Now that's irony; some might call it justice.

Plague 7: Hail
Exodus 9:13–35

Make no mistake, God is the Almighty God and He is to be worshiped. As He instructed Moses to say to Pharaoh, "Let My people go, that they may serve Me. For this time I will send all My plagues on you and your servants and your people, so that you may know that there is no one like Me in all the earth" (Ex. 9:13–14). From this passage, we see that God's purposes for the plagues were: (1) to show His power, and (2) to proclaim His name in all the earth (see v. 16).

God would elevate the intensity of the judgments with this seventh plague. This would be a hailstorm unlike any seen before in Egypt. Note that God calls them "My plagues." The false goddess Nut was supposed to be the god of the sky, and the false god Set (or Seth) was in charge of protecting against storms. Another false god, Osiris, was the god of agriculture, and this hailstorm would particularly focus on his realm of responsibility.

False gods are false. They exist only in the minds of the humans who conceive them. People create these gods because they desire to control some aspect of life, such as the basics of food or light or the desires of sex or wealth. They may create one god to have authority over a specific area, or they may create several gods to share the authority over that same area. When God battles them, He is battling with the minds of man. When He supersedes them, He is proving that the false god is no god at all.

When the Lord announced this plague, He also warned of its severity: "I will send a very heavy hail, such as has not been seen in Egypt from the day it was founded until now" (Ex. 9:18). He further warned the sons of Israel, "Bring your livestock and whatever you have in the field to safety. Every man and beast that is found in the field and is not brought home, when the hail comes down on them, will die" (Ex. 9:19).

By this point, some of the Egyptians were beginning to believe that God was the One Whom He claimed to be and that He could and would do what He said He would do. Some of Pharaoh's servants brought their slaves and livestock inside to escape the ravages of the storm. "The one among the servants of Pharaoh who feared the word of the LORD made his servants and his livestock flee into the houses" (Ex. 9:20).

When Pharaoh saw the severity of this electrical storm, he repented, saying, I have sinned this time, and then asked for forgiveness. One would think that he had found religion based on his next comment: "The LORD is the righteous one, and I and my people are the wicked ones" (Ex. 9:27). That attitude lasted as long as the storm; once it was over, he sinned again, hardened his heart, and refused to let the sons of Israel go to worship the Lord (see Ex. 9:35).

Plague 8: Locusts
Exodus 10:1–20

For the next plague, the Lord told Moses to once again emphasize to Pharaoh that He was performing signs so that the people "may know that I am the LORD" (Ex. 10:2). This time, He warned that He would bring swarms of locusts to cover the land. The locusts would descend and strip away any remaining green vegetation left from the hailstorm. Osiris, the false god of agriculture, was having a hard time with his crops.

By this time, Pharaoh's servants were getting fed up with his stubbornness and stupidity, and they advised Pharaoh to relent to Moses' demands. They said to him, "How long will this man be a snare to us? Let the men go, that they may serve the LORD their God. Do you not yet realize that Egypt is destroyed?" (Ex. 10:7). At first Pharaoh agreed, but when he discovered that Moses intended to take not only the men but also all the women and children and their flocks and herds, he changed his mind (Ex. 10:8–11).

So God directed an east wind to blow across the land all that day and all that night, and when morning came, the wind brought the locusts. The land was darkened. There had never been so many locusts in Egypt. Once again, Pharaoh repented, but after the destroying plague was removed, the Lord hardened his heart and Pharaoh changed his mind again. Thus the sons of Israel were not permitted to go.

Plague 9: Darkness
Exodus 10:21–29

This time, the Lord started off with the plague. The Egyptians had no advance warning of what was to come. The Lord told Moses, "Stretch out your hand toward the sky, that there may be darkness over the land of Egypt, even a darkness which may be felt" (Ex. 10:21). Moses obeyed, and three days of thick darkness fell across the land.

This was an attack on the false god Ra, the sun god, whom the Egyptians believed had control over light and darkness. Through this plague, God was demonstrating that there was no such thing as a god over darkness and light other than the true Creator God. At the beginning of creation, the earth was dark, and it was He Who had said, "Let there be light" (Gen. 1:2–3). God spoke it into existence. This time, He brought darkness. The true God was more powerful than the false god, and He was changing the minds of men.

This time, Pharaoh agreed to allow the Israelites to take the women and children with them, but he still stipulated that they were to leave behind their herds and flocks. But Moses replied, "You must also let us have sacrifices and burnt offerings, that we may sacrifice them to the LORD our God" (Ex. 9:25). The Lord hardened Pharaoh's heart, and he told Moses, "Get out of my sight! Make sure you do not appear before me again!" Moses told the Pharaoh, "Just as you say … I will never appear before you again" (Ex. 10:28–29 NIV).

Plague 10: Death of Firstborn
Exodus 11:1–10; 12:29–30

For the tenth plague, the Lord had Moses announce to the people, "About midnight I will go throughout Egypt. Every firstborn son in Egypt will die, from the firstborn son of Pharaoh, who sits on the throne, to the firstborn son of the slave girl, who is at her hand mill, and all the firstborn of the cattle as well" (Ex. 11:4–5 NIV).

Sure enough, it happened.

> At midnight the Lord struck down all the firstborn in Egypt, from the firstborn of Pharaoh, who sat on the throne, to the firstborn of the prisoner, who was in the dungeon, and the firstborn of all the livestock as well. Pharaoh and all his officials and all the Egyptians got up during the night, and there was loud wailing in Egypt, for there was not a house without someone dead.
>
> —Ex. 12:29–30 NIV

The Egyptians considered Pharaoh to be a god, and the firstborn son of Pharaoh, who was heir to the throne, was also considered to be a god. Isis, who was supposed to be the wife of Osiris, was the goddess charged with the responsibility of protecting children. Yet even with all of this supposed god-power, they were not able to overcome the real power of the real God. The Lord accomplished His purposes of showing His power and proclaiming His name through all of His earth (Ex. 9:16).

God proved He is sovereign. He governs all. He used the supernatural to demonstrate His power and wisdom, and He has done the same accordingly over the years. Let's get a little "taste" of that from other Scripture passages.

The Power of God

In Psalm 139:1–6, we are taught that God is omniscient:

O LORD, You have searched me and known me. You know when I sit down and when I rise up; You understand my thought from afar. You scrutinize my path and my lying down, and are intimately acquainted with all my ways. Even before there is a word on my tongue, Behold, O LORD, You know it all.

Psalm 139:7–12 teaches us that God is omnipresent:

Where can I go from Your Spirit? Or where can I flee from Your presence? If I ascend to heaven, You are there; if I make my bed in Sheol [the place of the dead], behold, You are there. If I take the wings of the dawn, if I dwell in the remotest part of the sea, even there Your hand will lead me … even the darkness is not dark to You, and the night is as bright as the day.

Finally, Psalm 139:13–16 teaches us that God is omnipotent:

For You formed my inward parts; You wove me in my mother's womb. … My frame was not hidden from You, when I was made in secret, and skill-fully wrought in the depths of the earth; Your eyes have seen my unformed substance; and in Your book were all written the days that were ordained for me, when as yet there was not one of them.

In the New Testament, we learn more about God's divinity and how He demonstrated it when He came to earth to live as a man. We know Him as the Lord Jesus Christ. On many occasions, Jesus claimed to be God: "I and the Father are one" (John 10:30); "He who has seen Me has seen the Father" (John 14:9); "Before Abraham was, I am" (John 8:58 ESV); "Your sins are forgiven" (Matt. 9:2).

In addition to making these claims, Jesus also demonstrated that He was God. His deity is confirmed again and again in the New Testament. One could point to many specific examples, but the gospel of John points out seven miraculous signs that Jesus performed (in addition to His resurrection) to prove His deity. These miracles show His authority over various aspects of life:

1. Authority over quality: Jesus turned water into wine (John 2:1–11). Jesus turned ordinary water into the best wine at the wedding feast at Cana.
2. Authority over distance: Jesus healed the official's son (4:46–54). Jesus was in Cana but healed the son who was twenty miles away.
3. Authority over time: Jesus healed the man at the pool of Bethesda (5:1–9). Normally, you wouldn't expect a person who had been sick for thirty-eight years, even if he were healed, to have muscles strong enough to pick up his mat. Yet in the time it takes to snap your fingers, the man was responding fully to Jesus' commands.
4. Authority over quantity: Jesus fed the five thousand (6:4–14). Jesus fed 5,000 people, plus women and children, with five barley loaves and two fish.
5. Authority over gravity: Jesus walked on water (6:16–19). Why wouldn't He sink in the water and drown?
6. Authority over disease: Jesus healed the man who was born blind (9:1–7). This man not only could not see, he was also born in that condition.
7. Authority over decay. Jesus raised Lazarus from the dead (11:38–45). At death, decay sets in and the body begins to stink. When Jesus ordered the stone to be removed from Lazarus's tomb after he had been dead for four days, Lazarus's sister Martha certainly expected there to be a bad odor that would come out. But Jesus restored Lazarus's body as well as his soul.

Just from these examples we can see that the Lord Jesus Christ has power and authority over quality, distance, time, quantity, gravity, disease, and decay. There are many other proofs of His deity recorded in the Gospels, but in reference to these seven miracles, the gospel writer states, "Therefore many other signs Jesus also performed in the presence of the disciples, which are not written in this book; but these have been written so that you may believe that Jesus is the Christ, the Son of God; and that believing you may have life in his name" (John 20:30–31).

Another portion of Scripture that demonstrates the Lord God is sovereign over all is found in the story of Job. In Job 38–41 alone, we read that God laid the foundation of the earth, placed boundaries on the sea, gave orders to the morning, knows the abode of darkness and light, reserves the storehouses of hail and snow for times of trouble, channels rain to desert lands, brings forth ice, governs the constellations, sends the lightning bolts on their way, counts the clouds, satisfies the hunger of lions, determines the duration of pregnancy of animals, unleashes wild donkeys, utilizes wild oxen, establishes the ways of an ostrich, gives strength to horses, directs the flight of an eagle, discerns justice, humbles the proud, made the behemoth, and subdues fierce animals.

It is interesting to note that when Moses announced the coming plagues to Pharaoh, in most cases the reason he gave for wanting Pharaoh to free the Israelites was so they could worship the Lord. The following verses are from the NIV translation:

- Plague #1: "Let my people go, so that they may hold a festival to me in the desert" (Ex. 5:1).
- Plague #2: "Let my people go, so that they may worship me" (8:1).
- Plague #4: "Let my people go, so that they may worship me" (8:20).
- Plague #5: "Let my people go, so that they may worship me" (9:1).
- Plague #7: "Let my people go so that they may worship me" (9:13).
- Plague #8: "We are to celebrate a festival to the LORD" (10:9).
- Plague #9: "You must allow us to have sacrifices and burnt offerings to present to the LORD our God" (10:25).
- Plague #10: The tenth plague was wrapped up in the institution of the annual Passover meal. The sons of Israel were to tell their children, "It is the Passover sacrifice to the LORD" (12:27).

God is truly sovereign over all, and He used the ten plagues to demonstrate His power over the Egyptian false gods. Yet He also used the plagues to demonstrate Who He was to the sons of Israel. Through the plagues, He revealed the Israelites' need to worship Him and trust Him.

Moving Toward Milk and Honey

At the beginning of the Egypt to Canaan pilgrimage, God's children, the sons of Israel, were taught Who the Lord is by means of the ten plagues. Believers today have several written reminders in the Scripture that also reveal the character and attributes of God. An ongoing study of the Bible will bless, illuminate, and encourage today's pilgrims who want to learn more about Who God is. It is an important beginning of the pilgrimage lesson, and it is an ongoing lesson. The future Milk and Honey Man would do well to study all about God. This is a powerful milestone.

CHAPTER 4

Passover

Salvation for the Milk and Honey Man

EXODUS 12:1–8

THE OLD TESTAMENT story of the Exodus describes the pilgrimage of the sons of Israel from bondage in Egypt to life in the Promised Land, Canaan, the land of milk and honey. Even though most Christians tend to focus on the New Testament and shy away from reading through the Old Testament—particularly a study of the development of the nation of Israel—there is much in the Old Testament that is instructive and applicable to Christians. This portion of Scripture spells out a pattern of development for the sons of Israel as they made their way to the Promised Land. As you study this story, look for things you can learn as examples of the Christian life. Remember, these things happened to them as an example, and they were written for our instruction. Have you missed any items of growth to this point? As we've stated, you are the potential Milk and Honey Man.

As we mentioned previously, all of the Israelites were in bondage from birth. No one was exempt. They needed deliverance, but they could not deliver themselves—only God could accomplish that. To be free from their bondage, they had to respond to God in faith. Likewise, the New Testament teaches that all are captive to sin. Paul writes, "All have sinned and fall short of the glory of God" (Rom. 3:23), and "None is righteous, not even one" (Rom. 3:10). This unredeemed condition is the reality for every person born into this world, and it is still the condition for those who have not yet been delivered from sin. The term "spiritual bondage" can be used to describe this condition.

In order to be set free from spiritual bondage, a person must first be exposed to the principle of sin and understand his bondage to it. Sin, as we stated, in essence means to miss the mark. It is like shooting an arrow and either missing the bull's-eye completely or hitting something other than the bull's-eye. As we read in Matthew 5:48, God's standard is perfection: "Therefore you are to be perfect as your heavenly Father is perfect." Sin is living beneath God's standards. Once a person realizes that he is in bondage to sin, he must then find a power source sufficient to deliver him. Is he powerful enough himself to effect that deliverance? No! That is why he is in bondage.

In the book of Exodus, God sends ten miraculous plagues that reveal His power over the false gods of Egypt. Through the execution of these plagues, God demonstrates that false gods cannot keep the Israelites entrapped and that He is able to deliver them. The true God is more powerful than all of Egypt's false gods.

The bondage of the Israelites and the demonstration of God's omnipotence are presented to future believers in order that they can understand their need for deliverance as well as the One they need to turn to receive that deliverance. At the point of salvation, people become "believers." They now fully trust God and belong to Him. In this chapter, we will examine that transition and how New Testament salvation is the fulfillment of the Passover in Exodus.

God's Deliverance of the Israelites

After God sent the plague on the firstborn against the Egyptians, He told the sons of Israel to begin preparations to leave Egypt. This would be the last plague against Egypt, and its devastating consequences would finally compel Pharaoh to agree to release the Israelites—including all of the women and children and their herds and flocks. The Israelites' deliverance was about to begin, and it would be marked by the event known as "Passover."

The New Beginning

"Now the LORD said to Moses and Aaron in the land of Egypt, 'This month shall be the beginning of months for you; it is to be the first month of the year to you'" (Ex. 12:1–2). A big change was about to take place in the lives of the sons of Israel, and it would begin with the establishment of the Hebrew calendar. In addition to celebrating Passover, the Israelites would also soon celebrate seven feasts of the Lord (Lev. 23) as part of that new calendar and that new life. The Lord was giving a new structure to the Israelites' lives throughout the year.

The same is true when a person becomes a Christian. He has a new beginning, a new birth, a new life, and he no longer follows the systems of the world. "If anyone is in Christ," Paul wrote, "he is a new creature; the old things passed away; behold, new things have come" (2 Cor. 5:17). This represents the occasion when a person becomes a Christian. This is his spiritual birthday. It is also interesting to note that God arranged for our calendar to revolve around the birth of Christ, adding "BC" for events before the birth of Christ and "AD" (*anno domini*, "in the year of the Lord") for events taking place after His birth. The Savior of the world had come. There was a new beginning for mankind.

The Lamb

"On the tenth of this month they are each one to take a lamb for themselves, according to their fathers' households, a lamb for each household" (Ex. 12:3). What is interesting here about the Lord's instructions is that the lambs were not limited just to sheep—goats were sufficient as well (see v. 5). The lambs of sheep or goats were used for sacrifices to pay for the sins of the people. There are several sacrificial lambs recorded in Scripture:

1. As we discussed previously, when Adam and Eve ate from the fruit of the Tree of the Knowledge of Good and Evil in disobedience to God's command, they sewed fig leaves together and made themselves loin coverings (Gen. 3:7). However, the Lord God clothed them with garments of skin (Gen. 3:21). The animal's blood was shed as a substitute for the penalty that was due them ("the wages of sin is death," Rom. 6:23). A lamb for a man.

2. In this first Passover, a lamb was killed in place of the firstborn son. When the blood was applied to both sides and the top of the doorframe of each Israelite home, the angel of the Lord "passed over" that home, and no firstborn within that home died. Only the lamb whose blood was shed died. A lamb for a family.

3. The Israelites observed the Day of Atonement each year, during which a lamb was killed and its blood sprinkled on the altar on behalf of the sins of the nation. A lamb for a nation.

4. The very first time John the Baptist first saw Jesus, he said, "Behold, the Lamb of God who takes away the sin of the world" (John 1:23). A lamb for the world.

Each of the first three lambs was a picture and a prophecy pointing to God's ultimate, permanently redemptive Lamb—His only begotten Son.

The Substitute

Notice that the lambs were a substitutionary payment for the penalty for sins because of peoples' disobedience to God. Again, the New Testament says, "The wages of sin is death" (Rom. 6:23). The term "wages" in this verse means something earned or deserved. When a person sins, death is the penalty he has earned. So, a slain lamb paid the penalty for Adam's disobedience to God. It was a substitute for the person or the people.

At the time of the first Passover, the Israelites were instructed to slaughter the lamb the night before they were to leave Goshen in Egypt to save the life of the firstborn in that house. Killing the lamb was a type, a picture and a prediction of the crucifixion of the Lamb of God, the Lord Jesus Christ. The lamb the Israelites chose had to be one without defect, to portray the sinlessness of Jesus. According to Hebrews 7:19, "(The Law made nothing perfect); and on the other hand there is a bringing in of a better hope, through which we draw near to God."

After Adam and Eve sinned, they knew they were naked and needed clothes, but the use of fig leaves was their own effort, and it was insufficient to cover their sin because blood had not been shed by the fig leaves (and "without the shedding of blood there is no forgiveness," Heb. 9:22). In the same way, we cannot be saved by our own effort. Adam had been told to refrain from eating from the fruit of the Tree of the Knowledge of Good and Evil or he would die. When Adam did eat the fruit, he began the process of dying immediately, and he eventually did die physically.[20] But Adam also died spiritually (inwardly) at the time he sinned; and the animal had to die to provide a blood covering for them. They accepted God's provision for them and were covered by it by wearing the skins as clothing.

In the garden of Eden, the animal that provided its skin for clothing was a substitute for the benefit of Adam and Eve. In Egypt, the lamb sacrificed at Passover took the place of the firstborn male of each Israelite family. In the New Testament, Jesus died for us—all of us, all nations—as our substitute, in order to deliver us from condemnation and the death sentence.

One of the best illustrations of Jesus' being a substitute is found in the life of Barabbas. He was a murderer who was headed for the death penalty, but the crowd persuaded Pontius Pilate to take Jesus instead. Jesus, the sinless substitute, died in the place of Barabbas, a murderer. Jesus, the sinless One, is also our substitute.

The Blood

In the days before I became a Christian, we visited a church where the preacher preached on "sin, and blood, and judgment." I came out of that service saying, "I don't need any of that!" Possibly you have heard someone ask, "Why do Christians talk about blood so much?" Or perhaps you have heard someone criticize Christianity by exclaiming, "Your religion is a bloody religion!" Why is there so much reference to blood in both Judaism and Christianity?

The reason is because life is in the blood. Leviticus 17:11 says, "The life of the flesh is in the blood." Physical life needs blood, and without it, no one can live. We are sustained physically by the blood flowing through our veins. Likewise, spiritual life is in the blood. Without the blood of Jesus, none of us could have spiritual life. We are sustained spiritually by the application of the blood of Christ that He shed on our behalf.

The Requirement of Obedience

The first nine plagues proved God's superiority to various false gods. The tenth plague dealt with the belief that a person could ensure his own posterity. Whether a king or a slave, men wanted a male child to carry on their family line. They, in effect, worshiped "the heir to the throne." But the Lord God is eternally king, and He alone holds that position. So the Lord established a plan that would show His power, would require worship of and obedience to Him, and would be a reference point and memorial practice for years to come. He instituted what He called "the Lord's Passover" (Ex. 12:11).

After slaughtering the lamb at twilight, the Israelites were to "take some of the blood and put it on the two doorposts and the lintel of the houses in which they eat it" (Ex. 12:7). He told the Israelites, "I am the LORD. The blood shall be a sign for you, on the houses where you live; and when I see the blood I will pass over you, and no plague will befall you to destroy you" (12:12–13).

The Passover lamb was a type of Jesus Christ, "the Lamb of God who takes away the sin of the world" (John 1:29). The Passover lamb was to be without defect, just as the Bible describes Jesus as being "without sin" (Heb. 4:15). He had to be perfect; otherwise, He would not have been worthy to pay the penalty for sin.

Note that for the Israelites to not suffer the consequences of the tenth plague, they had to believe that God could take their firstborn child's life in that way. God had provided the lamb as a substitute for shedding the blood of the first male in the family, but they had to obey God by putting the blood on the lintel and the doorposts. They also had to believe that the Lord was determined to take that course of action. Finally, they had to trust God sufficiently and believe that He would spare the life of their firstborn child if they followed these instructions. To their advantage, they had already witnessed God's judgment against the Egyptians' false gods on nine separate occasions. So they took the action and applied the blood as directed.

Their obedience served as an indication of their trust in God and an acknowledgement that He had the power to do what He said and that He would do what He said. It was an indication of their trust in Him for their deliverance. And the sign of their obedience was open for public display—all the Egyptians could see the blood applied to the doorposts and the lintel. The Israelites' testimony of their trust in the Lord was not something they could hide in a closet. God knew, which is why He passed over that family, and He knew that by following these instructions the Israelites were willing to tell anyone in the world that they trusted Him and were willing to demonstrate their faith by their obedience.

In the same way, as Christians, our obedience to God should be something we put on display to the world. God does not intend for us to hide our faith in a closet but to serve as an example to others of what it looks like to live as a follower of Christ in this world. We should also be willing to testify to the grace and mercy God has extended to us in giving us salvation.

The Penalty is Paid

When the Lord finished with the instructions about the Passover meal, Moses called together the elders and said,

> Go and take for yourselves lambs according to your families, and slay the Passover lamb. You shall take a bunch of hyssop and dip it in the blood which is in the basin, and apply some of the blood that is in the basin

to the lintel and the two doorposts; and none of you shall go outside the door of his house until the morning. For the LORD will pass through to smite the Egyptians; and when He sees the blood on the lintel and on the two doorposts, the LORD will pass over the door and will not allow the destroyer to come in to your houses to smite you.

—Ex. 12:21–23

Two things took place in Egypt that night.

First, the life of the firstborn of those Israelites who had obeyed God's instructions was spared. The firstborn was the representative of the family, and because all families traced their heritage back to Adam—both Israelite and Egyptian—they were guilty of sin (Rom. 5:12). God accepted the shed blood as a substitute and He passed over the Israelite homes of those who applied the blood to their doorposts. There was forgiveness.

Second, God delivered the Israelites from bondage. This took place the next morning. The people left the servitude to the Egyptians, and they took their riches with them.

While they were at Mt. Sinai, Moses gave the Israelites God's law, including instructions about worship. The Day of Atonement was established on the tenth day of the seventh month as a lasting ordinance. The high priest, Aaron, was to slaughter a bull for his own sin offering and sprinkle its blood before the ark of the covenant. Instead of justice (judgment), God would see the blood of the sacrificial lamb and extend mercy. Next, Aaron was to slaughter a goat for the sin offering for the people and sprinkle the blood on the atonement cover (Lev. 16). Again, as God saw the blood of the sacrifice, He would be merciful to the sons of Israel and would pass over them for a year. Their sins would be atoned and God was satisfied with the substitute.

We should note two things that also took place on Jesus' last day. First, Jesus' blood was shed for sin. Before He was crucified, He was scourged with a whip thirty-nine times. In that day, people often died from the amount of blood that He lost. Second, Jesus died for us. He was crucified for our sins. He did not die in the courtyard, but carried His cross part of the way to Calvary, was nailed to it, and died on it several hours later. The New Testament also teaches that "while we were yet sinners, Christ died for us" (Rom. 5:8). Jesus Christ took our place. He was our substitute. There was a penalty to be paid for our sins, and He paid the price for us.

Furthermore, the New Testament teaches that, "Much more then, having now been justified by his blood, we shall be saved from the wrath of God through Him" (Rom. 5:9). God used the shedding of Jesus' blood to justify us. Another expression of this is, "God presented him as a sacrifice of atonement, through faith in his blood. He did this to demonstrate his justice, because in his forbearance he had left the sins committed beforehand unpunished" (Rom. 3:25 NIV).

The angel of the Lord saw the blood on the doorpost, and it was sufficient for forgiveness—at least temporarily. In the new covenant, we are to realize our need and accept God's grace in His perfect lamb—whose sacrifice was once, for all.

The Significance of the Blood

What is the significance of the blood to God? Through Christ's death on the cross, the problem of our sin requiring judgment has been solved. We are forgiven! What is the impact of the blood on us? We don't have to feel guilty, because we realize the value of Jesus' blood. Two things happened when we accepted salvation: we were totally forgiven and we died with Christ. What is the impact of the blood on Satan? He makes charges against us, but the blood of Christ answers those charges. Those charges are invalid because of Christ's death and shed blood. Therefore, the blood has significance to God, to man, and to Satan.

Often, we struggle with the fact that when Christ died for us on the cross, the penalty for our sin was met. It is hard for us to understand the value of the blood and how it could redeem us from our sins. But we need to remember that the blood is for God, and He says that it is precious to Him (1 Peter 1:19). We must accept His value of it and accept God's plan of forgiveness by faith in our substitute. If God says the blood is acceptable payment, then we must agree, because God said it. The Israelites didn't say, "Besides putting blood on the doorpost we must do something else. That is not enough. That blood is from the lamb. We have to sacrifice a little bit ourselves." No, our value assessment of the blood must agree with His assessment of its value: paid in full!

Have you ever driven on any of the back highways of the South within a 250-mile radius of Chattanooga, Tennessee, and seen a barn with a sign on the roof or the side of the barn that read, "See Rock City"? The purpose of this sign is to tell the driver what to do: "Go to Chattanooga and see the attraction called Rock City." The person who painted the sign made it large so it would get the attention of drivers. It is intended to get the individual to take an action.

Now imagine a sign on the roof of the homes of the Israelites in Goshen in Egypt that said, "pass over this house." That is what the blood applied to the doorposts and the lintel was. The purpose of the blood was to tell the angel of the Lord to "pass over" that house and spare the firstborn of the family inside. The blood got the angel's attention, and each of the Israelite families in Egypt who applied the lamb's blood as instructed was spared.

Before the twenty-first century reader put his faith in the shed blood of Jesus Christ, his condition was that of being dead toward God. This is called "the old man" (or "old self"; Rom. 6:6 and Col. 3:9). That condition is symbolized in the following diagram by the black spirit in the center. Trust in the blood of the substitute was required for rebirth.

The Makeup of Man Before Salvation

*The Spirit
(Called "The Old Man")
is Dead Towards God.
Black – Totally Void
of Light.*

After man has placed his faith in the blood of the sacrifice, he becomes alive toward God. That condition is symbolized in the next diagram by the white spirit in the center. It is called "the new man" (or "new self"; Eph. 4:24 and Col. 3:10). Application of the blood to his life has made the difference.

The Makeup of Man After Salvation

*The Spirit
(Now Called "The New Man")
is Alive Towards God and
Indwelt by God's Holy Spirit.*

A Double Transaction

From this, we see that the first Passover in Egypt involved a double transaction: (1) The life of the firstborn was spared in the homes that applied the blood of the lamb to the doorpost and lintel, and (2) the Israelites were delivered from bondage. When the Israelites believed that the blood was sufficient for their salvation and acted upon that belief, it brought about their salvation. When the Israelites believed the Lord had delivered them from bondage in Egypt and acted upon that belief, they were able to leave Egypt and cross the Red Sea. Thus, they received both forgiveness and deliverance.

New Testament believers experience a double transaction as well. This double transaction pertains to forgiveness for the sins we have committed and deliverance from bondage to the power of sin. To explain the distinction, consider the following chart. The words "sins" and "sin" are listed on opposite sides of the cross shown in the figure below. This highlights the two aspects of Jesus' accomplishment when He suffered on the cross: (1) He died for our sins ("While we were yet sinners Christ died for us," Rom. 5:8); and (2) He died to the power of sin ("The death that He died, He died to sin," Rom. 6:10). All too frequently, the second point is omitted in the presentation of the gospel.

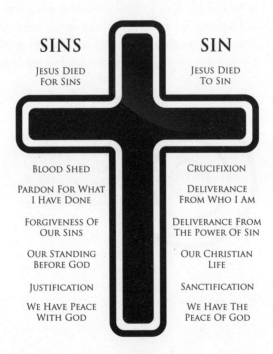

SINS	SIN
Jesus Died For Sins	Jesus Died To Sin
Blood Shed	Crucifixion
Pardon For What I Have Done	Deliverance From Who I Am
Forgiveness Of Our Sins	Deliverance From The Power Of Sin
Our Standing Before God	Our Christian Life
Justification	Sanctification
We Have Peace With God	We Have The Peace Of God

Jesus' blood deals with what we have done. His blood was shed to pay the penalty for our sins ("The blood of Jesus … cleanses from all sin," 1 John 1:7). Think of Jesus hanging on the cross at the point of near death because of the blood He shed. Jesus' death, however, deals with who we are. His crucifixion rendered sin powerless to rule our lives. Think of Jesus humbly submitting to God's plan of salvation ("Father, if You are willing, remove this cup from Me; yet not My will, but Yours be done," Luke 22:42), and then dying on the cross to achieve the ultimate victory over sin.

Jesus' shed blood bought and brought forgiveness of sins for those who trust Him. His death brought about deliverance from the power of sin for those who trust Him. Because of Jesus' blood being shed, believers standing before God are now justified ("We have now been justified by His blood," Rom. 5:9 ESV). Because of Jesus' death and our co-crucifixion with Him, in which we died to our former selves ("Having been buried with Him in baptism," Col. 2:12), our lives are now set apart for the Lord and we are sanctified.

Furthermore, because of our trust in the blood of Jesus being shed on our behalf, we now have peace with God ("Having been justified by faith, we have peace with God," Rom. 5:1); and because of our union with Him in crucifixion, we also have the peace of God ("And the peace of God, which surpasses all comprehension, will guard your hearts and your minds in Christ Jesus," Phil. 4:7).

Bob George provided a good illustration of this in his book *Classic Christianity*:

> The process of canning is an excellent illustration of the two parts of the gospel. Let's say that you are going to preserve some peaches. What is the first thing you have to do? Sterilize the jars. Why the process of sterilization? So that the contents of the jars—the peaches—will be preserved from spoiling.
>
> Imagine a husband coming home and finding his wife boiling jars in the kitchen. "What are you doing, honey?"
>
> "Sterilizing jars."
>
> "Why are you doing that?" the husband asks.
>
> "I just like clean jars," she answers.
>
> The husband is clearly at a loss. "What are you going to do next?" he asks.
>
> "Keep them clean!"
>
> This story doesn't make much sense, does it? You have never seen anyone decorate his kitchen with a sterile jar collection. No, the only

reason to sterilize jars is because you intend to put something in them. We would never expect to find a person involved in only half the process of canning, just cleansing jars. But we have done this exact thing with the gospel! We have separated God's sterilization process—the cross—from His filling process—Christ coming to live in us through His resurrection![21]

Map of the Pilgrimage

The following diagram is the second "chronological map" that compares the physical journey of the sons of Israel to the pilgrimage of the Christian life in the twenty-first century. At this stage they have completed their bondage in Egypt, witnessed the demonstration of God's power, and participated in the first Passover (which equates to the "crossing of the first threshold"). Notice that the map now includes a diagram for Mt. Sinai, which will be the next major stop in this stage of the journey to the Promised Land.

Applying the Blood

For the sons of Israel to be delivered, they had to believe that the application of the blood of the substitute, the lamb, on their doorposts and lintels would save the life of their firstborn sons. They also had to apply the blood as they were instructed. And the whole nation of Israel did so. They believed and obeyed and, as a result, they not only escaped the penalty of the plague but also were delivered from bondage in Egypt.

Do you have a substitute to pay the penalty for your sins? Have you been delivered from the bondage of sin? Do you know if you are going to heaven? Do you know that Christ wants to live through you? When the Israelites applied the blood to the sides and top of their doorframes, it wasn't their shed blood they were applying, but blood that was shed by a lamb on their behalf. Blood has also been shed on your behalf—Jesus' blood. Have you applied that blood? Have you received Jesus Christ as your Savior?

Trusting in Christ as your Savior requires you to be convicted of your sin by the Holy Spirit, to acknowledge your sin, to turn from that sin (repent), and to trust (believe) that Jesus Christ shed His blood as the payment of the penalty. The holy blood of the Lord Jesus Christ is the only sacrifice God accepts. Just as the sons of Israel in Egypt applied the lamb's blood to the doorposts and lintel of their homes, so sinners today must trust in the sacrificial blood of the Lord Jesus for forgiveness. It is God's only way. Jesus

CHRONOLOGICAL MAP
CROSSING THE FIRST THRESHOLD

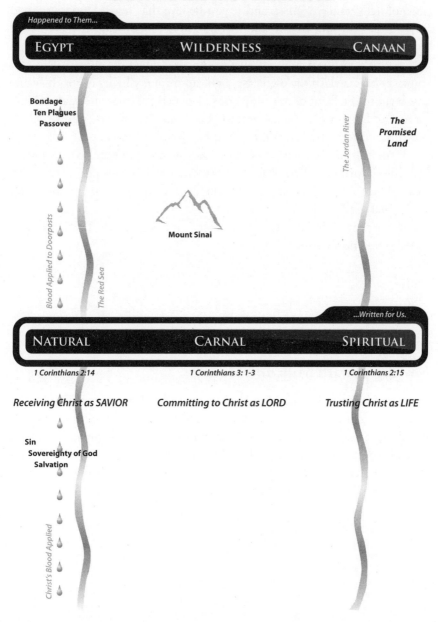

Happened to Them...

| EGYPT | WILDERNESS | CANAAN |

Bondage
Ten Plagues
Passover

Blood Applied to Doorposts

The Red Sea

Mount Sinai

The Jordan River

The Promised Land

...Written for Us.

| NATURAL | CARNAL | SPIRITUAL |

1 Corinthians 2:14   *1 Corinthians 3: 1-3*   *1 Corinthians 2:15*

Receiving Christ as SAVIOR   *Committing to Christ as LORD*   *Trusting Christ as LIFE*

Sin
Sovereignty of God
Salvation

Christ's Blood Applied

said, "I am the way, and the truth, and the life; no one comes to the Father but through me" (John 14:6).

If the Holy Spirit has convicted you of your sin and you realize your need of deliverance from it, and if you believe that Jesus' blood was shed for your sins on your behalf, and if you have never consciously placed your trust in Jesus Christ, then you can do so now. There are different ways that you can do this. Some pray a prayer; some walk down the aisle of a church; some get baptized. In my own case, I got up from my living room chair one day, went to the front door of my house, opened the door and said, "Come on in, Lord." However you accept the Lord, just be sure you know there is no work or merit you can add to complete Jesus' payment.

If you would like to receive Christ today, you might want to say a prayer like this: "Lord Jesus, I need You. Thank You for dying on the cross for my sins. I trust You as my Savior. Thank You for forgiving my sins and for giving me eternal life."

If you prayed that prayer, I encourage you to sign on the line below and to tell someone about it.

Your Name	Date

Moving Toward Milk and Honey

The Milk and Honey Man has three thresholds to cross before he can receive the abundant kingdom life that God has planned for him. The first threshold is the application of the blood of the Lamb. In applying the blood of the Lord Jesus Christ, the Milk and Honey Man accepts Him as his Savior and receives salvation. Only after he has placed his trust in Jesus as His Savior does he cross the first threshold and enter into the next area.

CHAPTER 5

The Pillar of Cloud
A Guide for the Milk and Honey Man
Exodus 13:20–22

WHEN THE EARLY settlers to America began to spread to the west, they often sent out a scout or engaged a guide who was experienced with the territory to lead them across the land. If you have ever travelled to a strange land and had no tour guide or street map, you know how difficult it can be to find your way. You need directions! The same was true with the Israelites. They were in a strange land and they had no way of finding their own way. So the Lord God provided a Guide for their journey.

> Then they set out from Succoth and camped in Etham on the edge of the wilderness. The LORD was going before them in a pillar of cloud by day to lead them on the way, and in a pillar of fire by night to give them light, that they might travel by day and by night. He did not take away the pillar of cloud by day, nor the pillar of fire by night, from before the people.
> —Ex. 13:20–22

It soon became necessary for this Guide to also become the protector for the Israelites. When Pharaoh learned that the sons of Israel had fled, he and his officials began to change their minds again. They said, "What is this we have done, that we have let Israel go from serving us?" (Ex. 14:5). So Pharaoh had his chariot made ready and began pursuing the Israelites.

> The angel of God, who had been going before the camp of Israel, moved and went behind them; and the pillar of cloud moved from before them

and stood behind them. So it came between the camp of Egypt and the camp of Israel; and there was the cloud along with the darkness, yet it gave light at night. Thus the one did not come near the other all night.

—Ex. 14:19–20

After the Israelites had almost completed crossing the Red Sea, the Egyptians came after them, but God protected them.

Then the Egyptians took up the pursuit, and all Pharaoh's horses, his chariots and his horsemen went in after them into the midst of the sea. At the morning watch, the LORD looked down on the army of the Egyptians through the pillar of fire and cloud and brought the army of the Egyptians into confusion. He caused their chariot wheels to swerve, and he made them drive with difficulty; so the Egyptians said, "Let us flee from Israel, for the LORD is fighting for them against the Egyptians."

—Ex. 14:23–25

In Psalm 48:14, the psalmist celebrated the greatness of God and His protection of His people, concluding, "For such is God, our God forever and ever; He will guide us until death." The prophet Isaiah also noted, "The LORD will continually guide you, and satisfy your desire in scorched places, and give strength to your bones; and you will be like a watered garden, and like a spring of water whose waters do not fail" (Isa. 58:9–11).

A Type of the Holy Spirit

The story of the Israelites' exodus from Egypt up to this point gives us a picture of the Trinity. First, God the Father heard the groans of the sons of Israel emitting from their bondage while they were in Egypt and he raised up a deliverer, Moses. God the Son, represented by the sacrificial lamb with no blemish or broken bones, shed His blood on their behalf. And God the Holy Spirit, represented here by the pillar of cloud, divinely guided them. The pillar of cloud could be considered a type of the Holy Spirit in several ways:

1. **The pillar of cloud guided the followers**. The presence of the cloud-by-day and the fire-by-night instructed the Israelites as to where they were to go at all times. That concept continues to be true for Christians today. "For all who are being led by the Spirit of God, these are sons of God" (Rom. 8:14).

2. **The pillar of cloud was provided as a gift for which the Jews had not asked.** The same was true of the Holy Spirit. Jesus said, "I will ask the Father, and He will give you another Helper" (John 14:16).

3. **The pillar of cloud was not provided to the Israelites until after they had exercised faith by applying the blood to the doorposts and lintels of their homes.** Likewise, today's new believer does not receive the Holy Spirit until, by faith, he believes that the Lamb of God (Jesus) was sacrificed for him.

4. **The pillar of cloud was used by God to speak to Moses and Aaron and, later, to Samuel** (Ps. 99:6–7). God frequently "came down in a pillar of cloud and stood at the doorway of the tent, and He called Aaron and Miriam" (Num. 12:5). The Holy Spirit also speaks to believers, giving them encouragement and guidance in their journey of faith.

The Guidance of the Holy Spirit

Thus, the first thing we notice as the sons of Israel begin their new lives is the provision of the pillar of cloud to guide them. Other passages in Exodus and Numbers give us further descriptions about the nature of the cloud:

Now on the day that the tabernacle was erected the cloud covered the tabernacle, the tent of the testimony, and in the evening it was like the appearance of fire over the tabernacle, until morning. So it was continuously; the cloud would cover it by day, and the appearance of fire by night. Whenever the cloud was lifted from over the tent, afterward the sons of Israel would then set out; and in the place where the cloud settled down, there the sons of Israel would camp. At the command of the LORD the sons of Israel would set out, and at the command of the LORD they would camp; as long as the cloud settled over the tabernacle, they remained camped. Even when the cloud lingered over the tabernacle for many days, the sons of Israel would keep the LORD's charge and not set out. If sometimes the cloud remained a few days over the tabernacle, according to the command of the LORD they remained camped. Then according to the command of the LORD they set out. If sometimes the cloud remained from evening until morning, when the cloud was lifted in the morning, they would move out; or if it remained in the daytime and at night, whenever the cloud was lifted, they would set out. Whether it was two days or a month or a year that the cloud lingered over the tabernacle, staying above it, the sons of Israel remained camped and did not set out; but when it was lifted, they did set out. At the command of the LORD they camped, and at the command of the LORD they set out; they kept the LORD's charge, according to the command of the LORD through Moses.

—Num. 9:15–23

Whenever Moses entered the tent, the pillar of cloud would descend and stand at the entrance of the tent; and the LORD would speak with Moses. When all the people saw the pillar of cloud standing at the entrance of the tent, all the people would arise and worship, each at the entrance of his tent.

—Ex. 33:9–10

Throughout all their journeys whenever the cloud was taken up from over the tabernacle, the sons of Israel would set out; but if the cloud was not taken up, then they did not set out until the day when it was taken up. For throughout all their journeys, the cloud of the Lord was on the tabernacle by day, and there was fire in it by night, in the sight of all the house of Israel.

—Ex. 40:36–38

In the same way, the first thing we see in the lives of newborn believers in Jesus Christ is the provision of the Holy Spirit:

But I tell you the truth, it is to your advantage that I go away; for if I do not go away, the Helper will not come to you; but if I go, I will send him to you. And He, when He comes, will convict the world concerning sin and righteousness and judgment; concerning sin, because they do not believe in Me; and concerning righteousness, because I go to the Father and you no longer see Me; and concerning judgment, because the ruler of this world has been judged.

—John 16:7–11

But when He, the Spirit of truth, comes, He will guide you into all the truth; for He will not speak on His own initiative, but whatever He hears, He will speak; and he will disclose to you what is to come.

—John 16:13

Moving Toward Milk and Honey

When you understand Who the Guide is and begin to follow Him, you will have passed another milestone toward your journey in becoming a Milk and Honey Man.

CHAPTER 6

Crossing the Red Sea
Baptism for the Milk and Honey Man
1 CORINTHIANS 10:1–5

WHEN THE SONS of Israel left Egypt and the Lord went before them in the pillar of cloud, He deliberately "did not lead them by the way of the land of the Philistines, even though it was near" (Ex. 13:17). The direction He led them was "around by the way of the wilderness to the Red Sea" (Ex. 13:18).

When the sons of Israel left Egypt, the starting point was the town of Rameses (Ex. 12:37). They went from there to Succoth, which means "booths" or "tents" (this could be a reflection of their future mode of overnight stay). However, the Bible does not say they "camped" there, so we do not know for certain whether or not they spent the night there.

From there they set out and camped at Etham, on the edge of the wilderness (Ex. 13:20). Next, the Lord instructed them to "turn back and encamp in front of Pi-hahiroth" (Ex. 14:2). This was so that the Pharaoh would think they were wandering aimlessly in confusion (Ex. 14:3). The Lord wanted to have another encounter with Pharaoh and, through that encounter, to be honored (Ex. 14:17). Furthermore, He was positioning the Israelites so that they had to call upon Him to get across the Red Sea. What looked like no planning or organization was simply a sovereign God directing His people for His purposes.

At this point, the Lord hardened Pharaoh's heart again, and Pharaoh ordered his army to go after the sons of Israel. "Then the Egyptians chased after them with all the horses and chariots of Pharaoh, his horsemen and his army, and they overtook them camping by the sea, beside Pi-hahiroth, in front of Baal-zephon" (Ex. 14:9). When the sons of Israel saw the Egyptians marching after them, they became afraid and cried out to the Lord. Moses calmed their fears and told them to, "Stand by and see the salvation of the LORD which He will accomplish for you today" (Ex. 14:13). The waters of the Red Sea were divided, and "the sons of Israel went through the midst of the sea on the dry land, and the waters were like a wall to them on their right hand and on their left" (Ex. 14:22).

Baptized into Moses

In 1 Corinthians 10:1–4, Paul said, "I do not want you to be unaware, brethren, that our fathers were all under the cloud and all passed through the sea; and all were baptized into Moses in the cloud and in the sea; and all ate the same spiritual food; and all drank the same spiritual drink, for they were drinking from a spiritual rock which followed them; and the rock was Christ." This passage in the New Testament is vital to understanding that the Israelites' pilgrimage, as recorded in the book of Exodus, represents a type in the believer's life.

In this passage, we see that the sons of Israel were baptized into Moses. What does this mean? Many definitions of the word "baptism" describe the method in which a person is immersed into water, but some also include the concept of being identified with something, as with a person, a group of people, or a message. For instance, the Israelites identified with their leader, Moses. Where Moses went, they went. What Moses did, they did. What Moses experienced, they experienced. Moses was their leader and initiator of their activities. The Lord told him what to do, and he led them in doing it.

Moses killed a lamb for his family; and the Israelites in turn each killed a lamb for their families. Moses put the lamb's blood on the doorposts of his house; they put the blood on the doorposts of their homes. Moses ate the Passover meal; they ate the Passover meal. Moses' family waited anxiously to see what would happen to their firstborn, and they learned that the sign of blood had been honored and their firstborn was spared. The rest of the sons of Israel experienced the same anxiety, and their firstborns were spared as well. All of this is very close identification!

Moses was chased by Pharaoh's army; the sons of Israel were also chased by Pharaoh's army. Moses had to trust the leadership of God manifested in a pillar of cloud by day and a pillar of fire by night; the Israelites also had to follow the same pillar of cloud by day and the pillar of fire by night. Moses had to walk through a path in the Red Sea with walls of water on each side, wondering if they would collapse; the sons of Israel walked through that same path with the same anxiety. That too, is very close identification!

In the book of Exodus, the sons of Israel obeyed God's instructions by cutting the throat of the sacrificial lamb and applying its blood on the doorposts and the lintel. Subsequently, they were led by God's representative through the Red Sea. (This represented baptism, even though not even their sandals got wet). The sons of Israel were "baptized into Moses in the cloud and in the sea."

The Israelites identified with Moses in every way.

Baptism for Christians

Christians are commanded to make disciples. In that process, we are also to baptize new converts. This is called an "ordinance" or an instruction from God. Jesus told His disciples:

> Go therefore and make disciples of all nations, baptizing them in the name of the Father and the Son and the Holy Spirit, teaching them to observe all that I commanded you; and lo, I am with you always, even to the end of the age.
>
> —Matt. 28:19–20

Water baptism does not make anyone a convert to faith in Christ; rather, it is an act performed by someone who already has received Christ. A person first becomes a Christian by receiving Jesus Christ as his Savior and then gets baptized in order to identify himself with Jesus, just as the Israelites came through the Red Sea and identified themselves with the God of Moses.

After the Lord Jesus shed His blood and died, His body was buried in the tomb, and three days later He was resurrected from the grave. The believing Christian acknowledges that the blood of Jesus was shed for him and identifies with the Lord Jesus through the act of water baptism. For the candidate seeking baptism, standing before the baptismal water is symbolic of Jesus hanging on the cross. Going under the baptismal water is symbolic of being buried with Christ, and coming out of the water is symbolic of being resurrected unto new life via Christ. By participating in the act of baptism, the believer is saying publicly that he has been "changed" (or "exchanged").

Because water baptism is not an act that produces faith in Christ, a person need not be distraught over the "proper" method of baptism. However, full immersion in water does serve as a better symbolic representation of identifying oneself with the death of Christ. Imagine if you were to put water in a bowl and then mix blue dye into the water. After this, you dipped your fingers in the bowl of blue water and sprinkled the water on a fresh white handkerchief. Then, using the same bowl and the same water, you placed another white handkerchief into the water in the bowl. This time, you immersed the handkerchief completely under the water.

If you compared the handkerchiefs, you would discover that the white handkerchief that had been sprinkled on had blue spots on it, while the handkerchief that had been completely immersed had turned solid blue—making it the same shade of blue as the water in the bowl. From this, you could say that the second handkerchief is fully identified with the blue water in the bowl. Some who support immersion say the method supports the concept of being totally dead on the cross, being wholly buried in the tomb, and being fully resurrected to new life in Christ.

This can help us understand the appropriateness of immersion as the method of baptism; however, it is important to remember that it does not make a person any more converted to Christ or a better Christian.

Identification with Christ

In 1 Corinthians 12:13, Paul states that at the point of salvation, a new believer in Jesus Christ becomes "baptized into one body" (or "in," "with," or "by" one body; the Greek preposition can be translated in different ways). Elsewhere in the New Testament, this is described as "the body of Christ." In other words, the believer becomes united and identified with Christ in death, burial, and resurrection. The "death" referred to here is a spiritual death, not a physical one. Death always brings separation. Physical death separates the body from the soul and spirit, while spiritual death brings separation between us and God. There are two aspects to spiritual death:

1. "You were dead in the trespasses and sins in which you formerly walked" (Eph. 2:1–2). Because of Adam, we were brought into this world separated from God. That is a spiritual condition. All of us were born dead spiritually.
2. "But God, being rich in mercy ... made us alive together with Christ" (Eph. 2:4–5). When we trust in Christ for salvation, God brings a change to our spiritual condition and makes us alive. Simultaneously, a different death takes place—we die to sin (Rom. 6:6–7). Initially, we were separated from God by the master called sin, but now we

are separated from that master. We still commit acts of sin and even have a drive to do so, but we are no longer under the mastery of sin. Those acts are what we have called "deeds of sin."

The New Testament refers to our former state before salvation as the "old self" (or "old man" in the Greek). This is the spirit of man, in which was found what we previously referred to as "inherited sin." But when we die to this old self, the former self is gone. As Paul states, it is "crucified with Him [Christ]" (Rom. 6:6) and "laid aside" (Col. 3:9).

Significant teaching about our identification with Christ can be found in Romans 6:3–10. In verse 3, Paul writes, "Or do you not know that all of us who have been baptized into Christ Jesus have been baptized into His death?" We have been identified with the Lord Jesus Christ, and when He died, we died (spiritually). Thus we were separated from "inherited sin." Because of this, "we have been buried with Him through baptism into death, so that as Christ was raised from the dead through the glory of the Father, so we too might walk in newness of life" (v. 4). We were united with Christ in baptism; thus, we were united with Him in death. Likewise, we were crucified with Him.

"For if we have become united with Him in the likeness of His death, we shall also be in the likeness of His resurrection" (v. 5). After Jesus died, He was buried. This burial proves His death, and we identify with it by partaking in water baptism. We also identify with Christ in His resurrection. The one follows the other. That is the new life. We can walk (live) in newness of life, believing, trusting, following, obeying, and walking by faith in the Lord Jesus Christ and His leadership. This does not mean we try to look good or try hard to be good. It means Christ is in us and wants to live His life through us.

"Knowing this . . . our old self was crucified with Him, in order that our body of sin might be done away with, so that we would no longer be slaves to sin, for he who has died is freed from sin" (vv. 6–7). Our old self has been crucified; therefore, we have been crucified with Christ. Death brings separation from all we were in life. It brings separation from sin and brings freedom from the master of sin.

"Now if we have died with Christ, we believe that we will also live with Him" (v. 8). Again, one follows the other. Spiritual death with Christ is followed by spiritual life with Christ. Christ is in us, and we are to yield ourselves to Him so that He can live through us. "Knowing that Christ, having been raised from the dead is never to die again; death no longer is master over him" (v. 9). Because of Christ's resurrection, He lives forever. Likewise, the believer in Christ lives with Christ forever and no longer has to commit sins.

"For the death that He died, He died to sin once for all, but the life that He lives, He lives to God" (v. 10). Jesus did not die for His own sin because He never sinned. He died for our sins and to the power of sin. He died once for all.

Moving Toward Milk and Honey

God used Moses to lead His people to the land of milk and honey. In following him, they were "baptized into Moses" and became closely identified with him in their pursuit of the Promised Land. In the same way, Jesus leads believers to the abundant, Spirit-filled life in which they are united with Christ. Believers identify with Him in His death, burial, and resurrection. Water baptism represents the believer's public statement of that identification with Christ. It is also a milestone in the journey to "milk and honey."

CHAPTER 7

Pharaoh's Army Drowned

Assurance for the Milk and Honey Man

Exodus 14

HAVE YOU EVER considered walking through the shopping mall of your town and shouting, "I'm going to heaven!" If you were to do this, you might find that a few of the shoppers would stop you and call you arrogant for thinking you were so good that you could go to heaven. But that would just mean they had the wrong plan of salvation. Salvation is not based on how good a person is but on having faith in Jesus Christ. If you have placed your faith in Jesus Christ, you could legitimately walk through the mall and shout, "I am going to heaven!" You would not be bragging, because your assignment to heaven is based on what Christ did, not on what you did.

But how can you be sure of that? A key verse in the New Testament is found in 1 John 5:13: "These things I have written to you who believe in the name of the Son of God, so that you may know that you have eternal life." From this, we see that it is possible for us to know that we will spend eternity with God.

Assurance for the Israelites

The Egypt to Canaan journey seems to teach that God's people can know they belong to Him and that He has in fact delivered them. After 400 years of bondage in Egypt and crying out to God, after seeing ten miracles performed by God through His servant Moses, after Pharaoh increased the burden by requiring the Israelites to get their own straw to make bricks, after the life of the firstborn in Egyptian families was snuffed out in the last miracle, and after the Israelites left the land of Goshen, they camped by the sea at Pi-Hahiroth. Once there, they could not get across the sea (Ex. 14:2). Subsequently, as we mentioned earlier, Pharaoh had a change of heart and "pursued the people of Israel while the people of Israel were going out defiantly. The Egyptians pursued them, all Pharaoh's horses and chariots and his horsemen and his army, and overtook them encamped by the sea" (Ex. 14:8 ESV).

The sons of Israel were fearful and said to Moses, "Is not this what we said to you in Egypt, 'Leave us alone that we may serve the Egyptians'? For it would have been better for us to serve the Egyptians than to die in the wilderness" (Ex. 14:12 ESV). But Moses said to the people, "Fear not, stand firm, and see the salvation of the LORD [that is, assurance of salvation], which he will work for you today. For the Egyptians whom you see today, you will never see again" (Ex. 14:13 ESV).

So the Lord commanded Moses, and he "stretched out his hand over the sea, and the LORD drove the sea back by a strong east wind all night and made the sea dry land, and the waters were divided. And the people of Israel went into the midst of the sea on dry ground, the waters being a wall to them on their right hand and on their left" (Ex. 14:21–22 ESV). As the Egyptian army chased the Israelites, the Lord looked down "on the Egyptian forces and threw the Egyptian forces into a panic, clogging their chariot wheels so that they drove heavily" (Ex. 14:24–25 ESV). Then the Lord instructed Moses to stretch out his hand over the sea, "that the water may come back upon the Egyptians, upon their chariots, and upon their horsemen" (Ex. 14:26 ESV). He did, and all of Pharaoh's army drowned in the sea.

The Israelites, even though they were frightened, obeyed God and walked through walls of water on dry land. They watched as the path through the water disappeared and the walls of water collapsed on the Egyptian army. At that point, they realized they were safe on the other side of the sea. They had arrived. They had assurance of their deliverance and believed because they saw it happen.

Assurance for the New Testament Believer

Assurance is an essential ingredient of personal Christian faith.[22] It is a sense of relief and freedom. It is confidence that the Word of God is true, that we will not experience judgment for our sins, and that we will spend eternity with the Lord. It is a sense of liberation.

Assurance results from belief. It is rooted in fact. It is knowing what the Bible teaches. It is knowing that Jesus is God; that He came to earth as a man, voluntarily died for our sins, was crucified and died, was buried, arose, and is seated at the right hand of God. It is checking the Bible out, finding that it makes sense, and experiencing God's intervention in our lives. Assurance is believing the facts.

Scripture says that God chose us before the foundation of the world, that we would be holy and blameless before him (Eph. 1:4). God provided His only begotten Son to die in our place in order to pay the penalty (which is death) for our sins. The Holy Spirit convicted us of our sinful condition, and we responded with faith (and even that came from God.) We acknowledged our sins (and our sinful state) and placed our trust in the Lord Jesus Christ. Like the sons of Israel, we did nothing to bring about our own deliverance; everything came from the Lord.

Assurance begins with the Word of God. Jesus said, "Your word is truth" (John 17:17), and that "if you continue in My word [read and study the Bible], then you are truly disciples of Mine; and you will know the truth, and the truth will make you free" (John 8:31–32). How can we know the Bible is truth? There are numerous arguments presented to support the claim that the Bible is true, but here is a brief explanation of two such arguments:

1. **The Bible is unique**. It was written over a 1,500-year span of time by more than forty different writers from different walks of life, including:

    •   Moses, who was brought up in the Pharaoh's palace by Egyptians;
    •   Joshua, a military general;
    •   David, a shepherd, a musician, a psalmist, a military leader, and a king;
    •   Solomon, David's son who became king after David;
    •   Nehemiah, a cupbearer and a governor;
    •   Jeremiah, a prophet;
    •   Amos, a shepherd;
    •   Luke, a doctor;
    •   Peter, a fisherman;
    •   Matthew, a tax collector; and
    •   Paul, a rabbi.

All these people contributed to the Scripture in different time periods. In addition, the Bible was written on three continents—Asia, Africa, and Europe—and in three different languages—Hebrew (most of the Old Testament), Aramaic (about half of Daniel) and Greek (all of the New Testament). Yet despite all these variations (and even more), the Bible is harmonious and unified. It is one unique message.

2. **The Bible contains fulfilled prophecy**. There are numerous instances in the Bible where a prophet of God depicted some future event that was to occur, and that event took place. For instance:

- Micaiah, a prophet of God, gave a near-term prediction that the wicked King Ahab would be killed in the battle with Ramoth-Gilead (1 Kings 22:17–28). Even though Ahab was disguised in battle, he was killed and Jehoshaphat lived (1 Kings 22:29–44).
- In the eighth century BC, the prophet Isaiah wrote that a king named Cyrus (his name was used in the prophecy) would be the leader who would allow the Jews to return and rebuild the temple (Isa. 44:28). Two hundred years later, Cyrus became king of the Persian Empire and allowed the Jews to return (Ezra 1).
- Isaiah also predicted that a virgin would bear a son named Immanuel (Isa. 7:14). This prophecy was fulfilled more 700 years later when Mary, a virgin, was found to be with child by the Holy Spirit (Matt. 1:18, 25).
- Around 700 BC, the prophet Micah wrote that the Messiah would be born in Bethlehem (Mic. 5:2). And He was (Matt. 2:1).
- In Psalm 34:20, the psalmist wrote that the Messiah "keeps all his bones; not one of them is broken." John 19:33 states, "They saw that [Jesus] He was already dead, they did not break his legs."[23]

The disciples and apostles knew the assurance that their faith in Christ had brought to their lives. In 2 Timothy 1:12, Paul wrote, "I know whom I have believed and I am convinced that He is able to guard what I have entrusted to Him until that day." In Romans 8:38–39, he also wrote, "I am convinced that neither death, nor life, nor angels, nor principalities, nor things present, nor things to come, nor powers, nor height, nor depth, nor any other created thing, will be able to separate us from the love of God which is in Christ Jesus our Lord." The apostle John taught this same assurance in the passage mentioned at the beginning of this chapter: "These things I have written to you who believe in the name of the Son of God, that you may know that you have eternal life" (1 John 5:13). In the same way, each of us as believers can have the assurance that we have been rescued from the bondage of sin and our former sinful state.

Moving Toward Milk and Honey

When you have assurance—when you believe that you indeed belong to the Creator of the universe—then you have passed another milestone in your journey toward becoming a Milk and Honey Man.

CHAPTER 8

Bitter Water
Health for the Milk and Honey Man
Exodus 15:22–27

AFTER CELEBRATING THEIR deliverance across the Red Sea and the demise of Pharaoh's army, the sons of Israel began their journey toward the Promised Land. They did not anticipate the stop at Mount Sinai or the "bumps" in the road that would come along the way. Yet God used these trials—these "bumps"—to train the Israelite pilgrims.

The first bump in the road came shortly after they escaped the Egyptian army. In order to get to the Promised Land, they had to cross the Sinai desert. The Israelites travelled three days and found no water. That got their attention! The Israelites were not accustomed to trials of this kind—daily brickmaking labor, yes, but unexpected lack of water, no. Their need for water provided them with the drive to find a place that had it. They came to the village of Marah, which had water. However, they were greatly disappointed when they drank it, for it was bitter. ("Marah" means bitter).

So there, in the Wilderness of Shur, the people "grumbled at Moses, saying, 'What shall we drink?' Then he cried out to the LORD, and the LORD showed him a tree; and he threw it into the waters, and the waters became sweet" (Ex. 15:24–25). To overcome the bitterness of the water, God performed a miracle. He used a tree to eliminate the bitter taste. This solved the problem and allowed the Israelites to drink the water.

The tree was God's solution to the Israelites' problem—and it is a solution for our problem as well. The tree is a type of cross on which the Lord Jesus Christ hung to pay the penalty for our sins. As Paul wrote in

Galatians 3:13, "Christ redeemed us from the curse of the Law, having become a curse for us—for it is written 'cursed is everyone who hangs on a tree.'" Christ hung on the cross (here called a tree), and we place our trust in Christ because He became a curse for us. Because of Christ, we are now forgiven and reconciled to God. Delivered from our old lives, we now trust Christ and are new creatures in Him. Although we are still in the world, we are no longer of the world or a part of it.

Just as the tree removed the bitterness of the water in Marah, so the bitterness of the circumstances in our lives are taken away by the cross of Christ. As Peter states, "He himself bore our sins in his body on the tree" (1 Peter 2:24 NIV). The cross of Christ heals the bitterness in life.

A Conditional Promise

Of course, when God delivers people from problems, He frequently accompanies His deliverance with some form of instruction. At Marah, God tested the sons of Israel by giving them a statute and a regulation. It was given as a conditional "if/then" promise: "If you will give earnest heed to the voice of the LORD your God, and do what is right in His sight, and give ear to His commandments, and keep all His statutes, [then] I will put none of the diseases on you which I have put on the Egyptians" (Ex. 15:26).

God performed ten plagues against the Egyptians through His servant Moses. These were plagues on a nation, and the Lord used them as judgment for the worship of false gods. At Marah, He promised not to put these plagues on the Israelites if they would hear and obey His commandments and do what was right in His sight. God informed the Israelites that He was the One Who heals (Ex. 15:26), and if they obeyed His instructions (recorded in Scripture), He would protect them from getting these diseases. This is where we get the name Jehovah-Rapha, "I am the Lord who is your Healer," as a name for God.

The Israelites had just proclaimed their faith in God by crossing through the Red Sea, but now they were unable to trust God with the provision of drinkable water. It should not have come as a surprise to them that God could handle the problem with the water at Marah. After all, He had just destroyed the Egyptians by means of His control of the water in the Red Sea. And if God could manage the waters of the Red Sea, He could surely be trusted to handle the waters of Marah. The sons of Israel, unfortunately, did not apply the faith they had so recently affirmed to their present dilemma.

In this passage, the bitter waters refer to bitterness in life, particularly those caused by health problems and diseases. In the book of Ruth, Ruth's mother-in-law, Naomi, lost her husband and two sons while in the land of Moab. Upon her return to Israel, she said, "Do not call me Naomi; call me Mara, for the Almighty has dealt very bitterly with me" (Ruth 1:20). Naomi was bitter because of her life circumstances and called herself "bitter" because of the bitterness of her heart. But the Lord blessed Naomi through her faithful daughter-in-law, Ruth. He gave Ruth a wonderful husband, Boaz, and a child, Obed, who was the grandfather of King David and, ultimately, ancestor of the Lord Jesus Christ. The Lord healed Naomi's bitterness.

God is still the great healer today. Yes, today much healing comes through God's provision of trained doctors and nurses, hospitals, and medication. However, make no mistake: be it by natural or supernatural means, the Lord is our Healer, our Jehovah-Rapha. Obedience to His instructions in Scripture will maximize the quality of our health.

Diseases that Cause Bitterness

Let's consider some of God's instructions concerning diseases that cause bitterness and the causes of those diseases. God gave this instruction to the Israelites, but they were written for our instruction as well. Some of these problems and diseases were more common at the time of the Exodus, while some are more obvious in our day.

> My son, be attentive to My words; incline your ear to my sayings. Do not let them not depart from your sight; keep them in the midst of your heart. For they are life to those who find them, and health to all their body.
> —Prov. 4:20–22

1. Leprosy

The Problem: From the Israelites in the wilderness to the mother of Ben-Hur at the time of Jesus Christ and through the "daily life of medieval humanity"[24] in the Dark Ages, leprosy has brought great fear to mankind.

God's Wisdom: "When a man has on the skin of his body a swelling or a scab or a bright spot … he shall be brought to … the priest. The priest shall look at the mark on the skin of the body" (Lev. 13:2–3). God instructed that those who showed signs of this skin disease were to be examined by the priest and then isolated if they were found to be contaminated to reduce the risk of the disease spreading from person to person. "He shall remain unclean all the days during which he has the infection; he is unclean. He shall live alone; his dwelling shall be outside the camp" (Lev. 13:46).

Solution: The isolation was a quarantine! And this was prescribed 3,500 years ago! The quarantine was used to reduce the spread of infectious diseases, which sometimes brought death. It has been effective ever since; over the years, doctors in various countries have used it to teach the need for cleanliness in many health situations. I first learned of leprosy when I watched the movie *Ben-Hur* starring Charlton Heston. This was the movie with the big chariot race in which Ben-Hur's opponent was trampled by the horses. Ben-Hur's mother got leprosy and was isolated with other lepers in a cave area. The isolation protected others from the spread of the disease.

2. Touching Dead Bodies

The Problem: Healthy people needed to be isolated from dead bodies because of the possibility of transferring disease from the dead to the living.

God's Wisdom: "Whoever touches the dead body of anyone will be unclean for seven days. He must purify himself with the water on the third day and on the seventh day; then he will be clean" (Num. 19:11–12 NIV). Throughout the Old Testament, from the time of Moses in 1400 BC to the time of the prophet Haggai in 520 BC (Hag. 2:12–17), the Word of God exhorted people not to touch dead bodies.

Solution: The wisdom of this command was evidenced in 1847 at the world's leading medical center at the time located in Vienna, Austria. It was discovered that many mothers of newly born babies were dying of "labor fever" (puerperal fever or puerperal sepsis).[25] The cause? Doctors were performing autopsies and then treating women in labor without washing their hands. In so doing, the doctors were transferring disease from the dead to the living. The problem only went away when the doctors consistently began the practice of scrubbing their hands after touching a dead body.

3. Burial of Dead Bodies

The Problem: Another cause of disease at the time of the Israelites was associated with the burial of dead bodies. When dead bodies were left out in the open, they started to decay and thus could readily transmit diseases.

God's Wisdom: "[A man's] corpse shall not hang all night on the tree, but you shall surely bury him the same day" (Deut. 21:23).

Solution: Today, some states expect burial, cremation, embalming, or refrigeration of the body of a deceased human by a specified time after a death. This helps to avoid the transmission of disease.

4. Sewage

The Problem: An improper system of disposing human waste can lead to an outbreak of cholera, typhoid, or dysentery.

God's Wisdom: "You shall also have a place outside the camp and go out there, and you shall have a spade among your tools, and it shall be when you sit down outside, you shall dig with it and turn to cover up your excrement" (Deut. 23:12–13).

Solution: In 1848, a cholera epidemic hit London, England, claiming the lives of 72,000 people.[26] It was discovered that the improper disposal of sewage was the cause of spreading the disease. At the time, the sewage from the city was simply dumped into the Thames River, which then contaminated the underground rivers that served as the city's main water supply. In time, the sewers were cleaned out, the river was cleaned up, and the drinking water was purified. As a result, the epidemic ended.

5. Alcohol Abuse

The Problem: Excessive use of alcohol poisons every organ of the body and causes damage to nerves and vital organs in the body such as the liver, the heart, and the brain. Those who are addicted to alcohol experience agonies when going through withdrawal, and pregnant mothers who abuse alcohol can cause damage to their unborn child. Abuse of alcohol can also cause sexual disorders.[27]

God's Wisdom: "Hear, my son, and be wise, and direct your heart in the way. Be not among drunkards or among gluttonous eaters of meat, for the drunkard and the glutton will come to poverty, and slumber will clothe them with rags" (Prov. 23:19–21 ESV).

Solution: In the New Testament, Paul told believers, "Do not get drunk with wine … but be filled with the Spirit" (Eph. 5:18).

6. Use of Tobacco

The Problem: Lung cancer is a well-known killer today. Smoking also causes cancer of the bladder, the pancreas, and the breast. Cigarette smoke thickens arteries, which often leads to heart attacks, and it contributes to male infertility.

God's Wisdom: The prohibition of tobacco use is not found in the Bible; however, present-day believers who read the New Testament are instructed, "Do you not know that your body is a temple of the Holy Spirit who is in you, whom you have from God, and that you are not your own? For you have been bought with a price: therefore glorify God in your body" (1 Cor. 6:19–20).

Solution: Like alcohol, nicotine is an addictive drug, and quitting is not easy. But if you want to prevent suffering from any of the various diseases and cancers caused by smoking, it is vital that you get help to quit.

7. Sexual Sins

The Problem: Sexual promiscuity can result in exposure to and contraction of various sexually transmitted diseases (STDs).

God's Wisdom: In Exodus 20:14, God told the sons of Israel, "You shall not commit adultery." In the New Testament, the writer of Hebrews stated, "Marriage is to be held in honor among all, and the marriage bed is to be undefiled; for fornicators and adulterers God will judge" (Heb. 13:4).

Solution: Today, not even "safe sex" has been successful in keeping people from contracting STDs. Staying with one partner for life is the much safer course.

8. Homosexuality

The Problem: It is reported that AIDS, gonorrhea, syphilis, and herpes are among the diseases that particularly affect the homosexual community. Furthermore, researchers have found that some mental health disorders, including suicide, depression, bulimia, antisocial personality disorder, and substance abuse occur at higher levels among individuals who practice homosexuality.[28]

God's Wisdom: "You shall not lie with a male as one lies with a female; it is an abomination" (Lev. 18:22).

Solution: Homosexuality is not a condition into which someone is born; it is a condition that a person can come out of. Those who want to do so should not be hindered from their choice for relief from these diseases.

9. Stress

The Problem: Emotional stress has multiple causes (e.g., anxiety about finances, employment, housing, safety, relationship with spouse, speaking in public, or grief from the loss of a loved one) and multiple manifestations (e.g., ulcers, high blood pressure, lack of menstruation, impotence, headaches, diarrhea, hives, obesity).

God's Wisdom: Proverbs 3:5–8 says, "Trust in the LORD with all your heart and do not lean on your own understanding. In all your ways acknowledge Him, and He will make your paths straight. Do not be wise in your own eyes; fear the LORD and turn away from evil. It will be healing to your body and refreshment to your bones." Psalm 37:3–4 says, "Trust in the LORD and do good; dwell in the land and cultivate faithfulness. Delight yourself in the LORD; and He will give you the desires of your heart." In the New Testament, Paul wrote, "Be anxious for nothing, but in everything by prayer and supplication with thanksgiving let your requests be made known to God" (Phil. 4:6).

Solution: Stress is a fruit of the flesh, while peace is a fruit of the Spirit. If you suffer from stress, it is important to meet with a doctor, counselor, pastor, or friend to examine what is going on in your life so you can make an adjustment in your thinking or actions.

10. Improper Diet

The Problem: Eating certain animal fats yields cholesterol, which makes deposits in the walls of arteries that can block the flow of blood. Over time, the blockage can shut off flow of blood through the artery, producing a heart attack.[29]

God's Wisdom: "You shall not eat any fat from an ox or sheep or goat" (Lev. 7:23).

Solution: To avoid diseases resulting from an improper diet, it is important to exercise and manage your dietary intake.

11. Revenge

The Problem: Dr. Stern asks, "Who is in control of your life—a spirit of revenge or the Holy Spirit?"[30]

God's Wisdom: "You shall not take vengeance nor bear any grudge against the sons of your people, but you shall love your neighbor as yourself; I am the Lord" (Lev. 19:18).

Solution: "The moment I begin to hate a man, I become his slave."[31] The solution to this problem is found in the second half of Leviticus 19:18: "Loving your neighbor as yourself" includes forgiving the person.

12. Anger

The Problem: Anger is a "significant factor in the formation of many serious diseases."[32] It can cause migraine headaches, neck spasms, ulcers, misery, depression, sickness, and contribute to accidents.[33]

God's Wisdom: "Cease from anger and forsake wrath; do not fret, it leads only to evildoing" (Ps. 37:8).

Solution: "Put to death, therefore, whatever belongs to your earthly nature … rid yourselves of all such things as these: anger, rage, malice, slander and filthy language … clothe yourselves with compassion, kindness, humility, gentleness and patience. Bear with each other and forgive whatever grievances you may have against one another. Forgive as the Lord forgave you" (Col 3:5, 8, 12–13).[34]

Wholeness Is the Goal

Although the information presented above comes from a variety of different sources, the primary source for this material is the book *None of These Diseases,* named after the Scripture in Exodus 15:26. The authors don't present the same subject matter as is in this book, but their bottom line is the same—wholeness is the goal. Here is how they close their book:

Only the Bible deals with the spiritual root of your problem.

"If we have been united with him like this in his death, we will certainly also be united with him in his resurrection. For we know that our old self was crucified with him so that the body of sin might be done away with, that we should no longer be slaves to sin. Rom. 6:5–6 NIV."

For Jesus, the path to resurrection had to go right through the cross. For you it is the same. Your path to new life runs right through the cross.

Every day you must escort your selfish, evil nature to the cross and there watch it die. Then you can experience the resurrection life in Christ."

- Death to self is the only way to inner peace.
- Death to self is the only way to inner spirituality.
- Death to self is the only way to deep joy.
- Death to self is the only way to claim God's promise, "none of these diseases …"[35]

I highly recommend the book.

The story of the sons of Israel at Marah provides us with an opportunity to learn how to live as a Christian. It provides us with a valuable lesson on the importance of living by faith, which includes being obedient. When the tree, representing the cross of Christ and all its benefits, was cast into the water, it healed the bitterness. The cross of Christ was applied to the problem and produced a resolution to it. In the same way, obeying the Scriptures applies the cross of Christ to potential medical and emotional problems in our lives. As believers, we are taught to obey; that is, to live by faith. Obedience is the evidence of faith, and if we believe that the Lord is Who He claimed to be and can do what He said, and if we trust Him, we will do what He instructed.

As believers, we are in the school of life, with the Lord Himself being our faithful and only teacher. As Paul stated, "The righteous man shall live by faith" (Rom. 1:17) and "whatever is not from faith is sin" (Rom. 14:23). Note that these passage do not say, "Christians shall get saved by faith," but just that they will live by faith.

The cross of Christ not only brought deliverance from the penalty for our sins but also brought death to the power of our inherited sin (Rom. 6:6–7). We have been forgiven of our sins, and now Christ lives in us to live through us.

Moving Toward Milk and Honey

The event at Marah was a milestone for the Israelites in the Egypt-to-Canaan pilgrimage. Likewise, learning to obey the Lord's instructions by faith is a milestone for the Christian in his spiritual growth.

CHAPTER 9

Manna

Food for the Milk and Honey Man

Exodus 16:1–36

AFTER THE LORD miraculously provided fresh water for the sons of Israel at Marah, Moses led them to Elim, where there were twelve springs and sixty palm trees (Ex. 15:27). It would be the last respite for the Israelites for some time, for Moses would now prove his faith in the Lord by leading them into the Wilderness of Sin. Every step they took would now lead them away from places of provisions. Interestingly, Moses knew about the wilderness, as he had lived there for forty years, but it is likely that he did not expect the trials they would encounter. Moses was simply following the Cloud and trusting in the Lord.

The sons of Israel were headed for the Promised Land, but when they came to the Wilderness of Sin, they began to grumble against Moses and Aaron because of their hunger. "Would that we had died by LORD's hand in the land of Egypt," they grumbled, "when we sat by the pots of meat, and when we ate bread to the full" (Ex. 16:3). Then the Lord said, "Behold, I will rain bread from heaven for you" (Ex. 16:4). And He did. After all, He had promised the Israelites that they would worship Him at Mt. Sinai (Ex. 3:12), and He wasn't going to let them die of hunger along the way.

The next morning, when the layer of dew evaporated, the sons of Israel saw that there was "a fine flake-like thing, fine as the frost on the ground" (Ex. 16:14). When the people asked, "What is it?" Moses responded, "It is the bread which the LORD has given you to eat" (Ex. 16:15). The Israelites called the flake-like substance "manna," which means, "what is it?" (Ex. 16:31).

Some 450 years later, the psalmist recounted these works of the Lord on behalf of His people when he wrote, "He rained down manna upon them to eat and gave them food from heaven. Men did eat the bread of angels; He sent them food in abundance" (Ps. 78:24–25). And some 550 years after that, Nehemiah also reported God's faithful care of the sons of Israel, saying, "You provided bread from heaven for them for their hunger" (Neh. 9:15).

Once again, however, this miracle included another lesson in obedience for the Israelites. God instructed the people to gather only a day's portion each day, and then, on the sixth day, to gather twice as much as they gathered daily, as they were not to pick up manna on the Sabbath. Of course, this supported the Lord's instruction prohibiting work on the Sabbath. The sons of Israel were being tested by God—to "test them whether they will walk in my law or not" (Ex. 16:4 ESV).

Despite God's command, some of the people still went out to gather manna on the Sabbath—and, of course, they found none. At this point, the Lord said to Moses, "How long will you [the people of Israel] refuse to keep my commandments and my laws? See! The LORD has given you the Sabbath; therefore on the sixth day he gives you bread for two days. Remain each of you in his place; let no one go out of his place on the seventh day" (Ex. 16:27–29 ESV). So, after this, the people rested on the Sabbath (Ex. 16:30).

From Physical to Spiritual

In John 6:48–51 (ESV), Jesus said, "I am the bread of life. Your fathers ate the manna in the wilderness, and they died. This is the bread that comes down from heaven, so that one may eat of it and not die. I am the living bread that came down from heaven. If anyone eats of this bread, he will live forever. And the bread that I will give for the life of the world is my flesh."

What Jesus was saying was that the Israelites' experience of eating manna in the wilderness was a physical happening. They were hungry, so they cried out to God, and He provided them sustenance. Everyone must have physical food to sustain physical life. However, believers must also have spiritual food to sustain spiritual life. This type of food, the "bread of life," comes only from Christ. Jesus is the bread of life, and those who partake of His flesh shall live forever.

The fact that the Jewish leaders did not understand the spiritual lesson Jesus was presenting here is evidenced by their next question: "How can this man give us his flesh to eat?" (John 6:52 ESV). They thought He was talking about a physical matter. In fact, when Jesus spoke about His flesh, He was referring to the fact that He would die—that is, give up His flesh—on the cross for our behalf. If we believe in Him and trust in His death on the cross on our behalf, we will gain eternal life.

From this, we learn that just as there is a hunger for physical food, there is also a hunger for spiritual food. The Bible—the written Word of God—feeds us spiritual food; it is truth. Jesus is the living Word of God, and we are to "eat His flesh." Have you ever prayed before eating a meal, "Thank You, Lord, for this food; we ask you to nourish our bodies"? It is also appropriate to pray before reading the Bible, "Thank You, Lord, for this food; we ask you to nourish our souls."

In 1 Corinthians 10:1–3, Paul wrote, "Our fathers … all ate the same spiritual food" (ESV). The sons of Israel, the "believers" of the Exodus, ate manna for forty years in the wilderness (Ex. 16:35). But New Testament believers have a different spiritual food: Jesus!

The Bread of Life

Just before Jesus began His discussion on the bread of life in John 6:48–51, He performed the miracle of the feeding of the 5,000. Once the crowd who participated in the miracle had filled their stomachs, Jesus withdrew from them and went to the mountain by Himself (John 6:15). When evening came, His disciples went down to the sea and started across it, heading toward Capernaum. As they were making their way across, Jesus came out to them, walking on the sea.

When the disciples saw Him, they thought He was a ghost and cried out in fear. But Jesus immediately spoke to them and said, "It is I; do not be afraid" (John 6:20). Mark's gospel describes this same incident, but adds that the disciples "did not understand about the loaves, but their hearts were hardened" (Mark 6:52 ESV). By "hearts," Mark was not talking about the physical organ that pumps blood for physical life, but the spiritual organ that pumps blood for spiritual life, eternal life.

The crowd who had participated in the miracle the previous day did not participate with the disciples in Jesus' walking on the Sea of Galilee. However, they apparently suspected something miraculous had occurred, because they saw "that there had been only one boat" on the eastern shore of the Sea of Galilee and that "Jesus had not entered the boat with his disciples" (John 6:22 ESV). So the crowds went in search of Him.

When they found Him in Capernaum, they asked, "When did You get here?" (John 6:25). By this, they probably meant, "How did you get here?" Jesus turned the question from when (or how) to why they were searching for Him—and then He answered the question Himself. He told them they were not looking for Him to see a miracle but to find out how to get their stomachs filled. In two sentences, Jesus changed the question into a lesson on salvation and sanctification and how to obtain it. It was not about filling their stomachs, but about filling their hearts. Jesus took what happened to them and turned it into what was written for us.

The Request for a Sign

When God provided the sons of Israel with manna in the desert, it was for the purpose of proving that He would provide physical life for them if they would learn to depend on Him. For the sons of Israel, that was a pursuit of filling their stomachs. For the crowds who had gone searching for Jesus, however, He was providing them with the essentials for eternal life. Jesus—the Bread of Life—was certified by God to provide them with this life (John 6:37). Furthermore, this eternal life was not just a one-time event of "getting saved" or "going to heaven." One who is saved has eternal life now, and the benefits are to be realized, developed, and used in this life on an ongoing basis.

When those in the crowd recognized Jesus' claim of authority and His claim of qualifications, they asked Him what was required to be "doing the works of God" (John 6:28 ESV). Jesus said they had to believe in (and trust in on an ongoing basis) the person whom God had sent (Himself). At this point, they wanted proof He was the One. "What sign [miracle] do you do, that we may see and believe you?" they asked (John 6:30 ESV). The crowd already knew Jesus could perform miracles. In fact, they were "following Him, because they saw the signs" (John 6:2 ESV)—and that was before the feeding of the 5,000. Their request—no, demand—for another miracle reflected their hardness of heart and their spiritual blindness.

Disbelief is never satisfied. No matter how many facts or how many miracles a disbelieving person witnesses, he will never see the truth until the Lord quickens his spirit. He will never see Who Jesus really is. One more miracle is just not going to do it.

So we see that while Moses led a nation of two to three million people and provided bread from heaven for them, Jesus made the Bread of Life available to the entire world. While the Israelites had to depend upon God to meet their physical needs for food, those who desire the Bread of Life to meet their spiritual needs must depend upon Christ. Salvation is by grace alone (Eph. 2:8–9), through faith alone (Rom. 3:28), and in Christ alone (Acts 4:12).

The followers of Jesus would never go hungry and never be thirsty (John 6:35). Because of their belief in Jesus, they would have eternal life, and He promised to raise them up on the last day. The "sign seekers," on the other hand, would never believe and thus would never receive the Bread of Life Jesus was offering to them, because they had hard hearts. And the Israelite establishment grumbled against Jesus. They had much to learn and would need to be taught by God. They could not come to Jesus unless they were drawn by the Father.

Moving Toward Milk and Honey

Jesus is the antitype of manna; He is the Bread of Life. He has commanded us to "eat His flesh," which is a spiritual figure of speech that means we are supposed to study and trust the Word of God. Jesus is the living Word of God, and the Bible is the written Word of God. Thus, we are supposed to study the Bible. When you begin a program of regular Bible study, you will have passed another milestone in your journey toward becoming a Milk and Honey Man.

CHAPTER 10

Strike the Rock
Water for the Milk and Honey Man
EXODUS 17:1–7

AFTER THE ISRAELITES' experience in the Wilderness of Sin, the Lord again led His people to a place with a water problem. Ironically, the name of the place was "Rephidim," which means "refreshments." The name had been assigned to the place years before. Would it live up to its prophecy?

For the sons of Israel, this provided yet another opportunity to trust the Lord's willingness to provide and His ability to do so. The Lord had previously proven He could handle water. He parted the waters of the Red Sea, He returned the water and drowned the Egyptian army, and He removed the bitterness of the water at Marah. He had also proven He could provide food for the Israelites when He gave them manna and quail in the Wilderness of Sin.

The incident at Rephidim was just another bump in the road along the journey—just another trial of their trust in God. How would the Israelites respond to this test?

Striking the Rock

Even though the sons of Israel had previously tested the Lord and found Him to be faithful to them, they once again demonstrated their lack of faith in Him. When they saw there was no water at the place, they immediately began to grumble and argue with God's representative, Moses. In doing so, they failed God's test of whether or not they would trust Him—of whether or not they would live by faith.

When the people began to quarrel with Moses, he rebuked them (Ex. 17:2). The Israelites grumbled, Moses prayed, and the Lord gave Moses instructions (Ex. 17:3–6), telling them to take some of the elders of Israel with him, go to the rock at Horeb, and strike the rock with his staff. So Moses took the elders, the leaders in the tribes, with him to the rock at Horeb. Then he did what the Lord instructed "in the sight of the elders of Israel" (Ex. 17:6). The elders present thus served as credible witnesses to the Israelites of the miraculous event that was to occur.

In Exodus 4:20, Moses' staff is called the "staff of God." It was the same staff Moses used to strike the Nile River, divide the Red Sea, and perform other signs. It was a symbol of God's power, and holding it was a sign of dependence and trust in God. With this staff, Moses now struck the rock at Horeb, and water came out of it in abundance. Subsequently, Moses gave new names for that location: "Massah" (which means "test") and "Meribah" (which means "quarrel"). These names were used to remind the sons of Israel of the experience.

The real test for the Israelites was whether the Lord was among them or not (Ex. 17:7). What did they find out? They found that God was with them constantly. He proved it again by providing the water at Rephidim.

The New Testament states that "the rock was Christ" (1 Cor. 10:4). The rock at Horeb was the type; Jesus was the fulfillment. Moses' striking the rock at Horeb was a symbol of God's judgment; striking the rock symbolically refers to Jesus' crucifixion. He was judged for our sins, and because He paid our penalty, any who trust Him for salvation are therefore "paid up" and no longer guilty. At Rephidim the water did not come out until the rock was struck. Likewise, the gospel of grace was not sent forth until Jesus was crucified.

The Lesson of Massah/Meribah in Psalm 95

More than 400 years after the sons of Israel's experience at Massah/Meribah, the psalmist penned the words of Psalm 95 to reflect on the event. Below is an explanation of verses 7c–11.

Verses 7c and 8a—The Call to Trust God

"Today, if you would hear his voice, do not harden your hearts …" Even after 400 years, the people of Israel remembered that their forefathers had "disbelieved" and failed to trust in God, and this failure was recorded in passages such as Psalm 95.

Verses 8b and 9—The Example of Failure to Trust God

"Do not harden your hearts as at Meribah, as in the day of Massah in the wilderness, When your fathers tested Me, they tried Me, though they had seen My work." Here, the psalmist gives a warning about failing to trust in God. Meribah means "quarreling" and Massah means "testing." At this location, Meribah and Massah, the sons of Israel quarreled and tested God—and this in spite of the fact that they had seen the ten plagues, the parting of the Red Sea, and the miraculous provision of water and food. They had seen God's work.

Verses 10 and 11—The Result of Failure to Trust God

"For forty years I loathed that generation, and said they are a people who err in their heart, they do not know My ways. Therefore I swore in My anger, truly they shall not enter into My rest."

Here the psalmist jumps to another incident that occurred slightly more than a year later when the twelve spies voted ten to two to forsake trust in God and the whole nation was punished with forty years of wandering in the wilderness. In His anger, God swore that that generation of Israelites (except for Joshua and Caleb) would not enter the Promised Land. Those who trusted God could go in; the others could not.

What is God's rest? For the sons of Israel, it was a place—but it was a place that to enter required a certain approach to life. It required lifestyle of trusting in God to direct their lives and resting in the knowledge that He would do so on a daily basis. He is the boss, the decision maker, and He is the One doing the work. That applies for us today as well. It is leading a faith-led, Spirit-filled life. As the apostle Paul affirms in Romans 1:17, "The righteous man shall live by faith."

Jesus Quenches Thirst

In 1 Corinthians, Paul used the term "spiritual" to refer to those things that are produced by the Holy Spirit. For example, "spiritual gifts" are the gifts that the Spirit gives (1 Cor. 12:1). In the same way, the "spiritual food" and "spiritual drink" of the Israelites was the water and manna God provided (1 Cor. 10:3), and they all drank from the "spiritual rock" (1 Cor. 10:4), which Paul likened to our Lord, Who miraculously accompanied His people.

In John 7, Jesus attended the Feast of the Tabernacles in Judea. On the last day of the feast, Jesus stood and cried out, "If any one is thirsty, let him come to Me and drink. He who believes in Me, as the Scripture said, 'From his innermost being will flow rivers of living water'" (v. 38). The Jews had a ceremony of carrying water from the Pool of Siloam and pouring it into a silver basin in the altar of burnt offering for the first seven days of the Feast of Tabernacles. On the eighth day this was not done, making Christ's offer of the water of eternal life from Himself even more startling.

Jesus' offer of living water was both a principle and an invitation. In John 4, the apostle John revealed the effectiveness of pursuing this living water in a story known as "the woman at the well." Jesus was travelling through Samaria when He came to a place called Jacob's well. When a Samaritan woman came to draw water, Jesus said to her, "Give Me a drink" (v. 7). The woman replied, "How is it that You, being a Jew, ask me for a drink since I am a Samaritan woman?" (At the time, the Jews did not associate with the Samaritans.)

Jesus answered, "If you knew the gift of God, and who it is who says to you, 'Give Me a drink,' you would have asked Him, and he would have given you living water" (v. 10).

"Sir," the woman said, "You have nothing to draw water with and the well is deep; where then do you get that living water? You are not greater than our father Jacob, are You, who gave us the well, and drank of it himself and his sons and his cattle?" (vv. 11–12).

"Everyone who drinks of this water will thirst again; but whoever drinks of the water I will give him will never thirst; but the water that I will give him will become in him a well of water springing up to eternal life," Jesus said (vv. 13–14).

The woman then asked Him to give her this water, so that she would "not be thirsty, nor come all the way here to draw" (v. 15).

We must rely on the Lord to supply our necessities in life, like food and water. If we believe electricity will work and that it will cause the light in our room to come on when we flip the light switch, then we should be able to believe we can receive necessary provisions when we trust the creator of those provisions.

Moving Toward Milk and Honey

The Lord brought the sons of Israel to the place where their faith would be tested. This event was so significant that the Lord recorded it in Psalms and again in the New Testament in the book of Hebrews. This failure of the Israelites' faith during their pilgrimage to Canaan was an important (though negative) event, and therefore was a milestone for the sons of Israel. This event was recorded to serve as an example for us, and we must learn from it. We will encounter various tests of our faith during our Christian walk, and we must learn through our failures and our successes. When we do, it represents a milestone in our lives.

CHAPTER 11

Amalek
The Battle of the Flesh and the Spirit
Exodus 17:8–16

AFTER THE LORD miraculously provided water to the sons of Israel, they were attacked by the nation of Amalek (the Amalekites). This would turn out to be an ongoing battle between the two nations and would present an obstacle to success in the pilgrimage of the chosen people.

During one such instance, when Moses saw the Amalekites approach at Rephidim, he said to his servant Joshua, "Choose men for us and go out, fight against Amalek. Tomorrow I will station myself on the top of the hill with the staff of God in my hand" (Ex. 17:9). So Joshua fought the Amalekites as Moses ordered, while Moses, Aaron, and Hur went up to the top of the hill. "So it came about when Moses held his hand up [representative of trusting the Lord], that Israel prevailed, and when he let his hand down, Amalek prevailed" (vv. 10–11). When Moses' hands grew tired, they took a stone and put it under him, and he sat on it. Then Aaron and Hur held his hands up—one on either side—so that they would remain steady until sunset. In this way, Joshua was able to overcome the Amalekite army. Trusting in God brought the victory.

An Ongoing Battle

After the battle, Moses built an altar and called it "The LORD is my Banner." Then he said, "The LORD will have war against Amalek from generation to generation" (Ex. 17:15–16). Sure enough, it happened. Years later after Israel had settled in the Promised Land and Saul was their king, the prophet Samuel came to him and said,

> The LORD sent me to anoint you as king over His people, over Israel; now therefore, listen to the words of the LORD. Thus says the LORD of hosts, "I will punish Amalek for what he did to Israel, how he set himself against him on the way [to the Promised Land] while he was coming up out of Egypt. Now go and strike Amalek and utterly destroy all that he has, and do not spare him; but put to death both man and woman, child and infant, ox and sheep, camel and donkey."
>
> —1 Sam. 15:1–3

Saul did destroy the Amalekites, but not completely. Instead, he kept the "best" part for himself.

> [King Saul] captured Agag the king of the Amalekites alive, and utterly destroyed all the people with the edge of the sword. But Saul and the people spared Agag and the best of the sheep, the oxen, the fatlings, the lambs, and all that was good, and were not willing to destroy them utterly; but everything despised and worthless, that they utterly destroyed.
>
> —1 Sam. 15:8–9

In the battles with the Amalekites, the nation of Amalek was a type of "the flesh," and the battle with the Israelites was a type of the battle of the "flesh and the spirit" with which Christians constantly struggle (Gal. 5:17). When we are called on to utterly destroy the flesh, we often fall into the same trap as Saul. Aren't we the same way today?

Don't we save the best of the flesh and try to use it—and even try to dedicate it to God? "Lord, these are my spiritual gifts, and because they are spiritual gifts, it must mean that You gave them to me. Therefore, they must be spiritual, not fleshly … so I will use them for You, Lord."

But God says, "You can do anything by the power of the flesh. I want to decide what gifts are to be used and when—and I want to be the One Who uses them."

When King Saul and the prophet Samuel next met, Saul told the prophet he had carried out the Lord's instructions. Samuel replied, "What then is this bleating of the sheep in my ears, and the lowing of the oxen which I hear?" (1 Sam. 15:14).

To defend his actions, Saul said, "They [blaming the people] have brought them from the Amalekites, for the people spared the best of the sheep and oxen, to sacrifice to the LORD your God; but the rest we [now taking credit] have utterly destroyed" (v. 15).

When Saul kept up his self-defense, Samuel replied, "Has the LORD as much delight in burnt offerings and sacrifices as in obeying the voice of the LORD? Behold, to obey is better than sacrifice, and to heed than the fat of rams. 'For rebellion is as the sin of divination, and insubordination is as iniquity and idolatry. Because you have rejected the word of the LORD, He has also rejected you from being king'" (vv. 22–23). Subsequently, Samuel "hewed Agag to pieces before the LORD in Gilgal" (v. 33).

The battle with the flesh went on from generation to generation just as Moses had promised. About 1,000 years later, when the Israelites were living in exile in Persia, they received an attack from a man named Haman. Haman's father was an Agagite, a descendant of King Agag (king of the Amalekites), and he came up with a plot to have all the Jews put to death (Est. 3:1–6). Esther, the new queen, who was an Israelite, interceded on the Jews' behalf. She called for prayer and fasting, giving evidence of her trust in Jehovah God. As a result, the sons of Israel were delivered, giving evidence of the power of faith over flesh.

The Makeup of Man

We have already seen that there are some differences between the specifics for God's people in the Old Testament and the New Testament. So at this juncture, it might be helpful to review the makeup of man.

As we discussed in Chapter 2, some people describe man as being composed of material and immaterial parts (the body being the material part). This could be described as the "dichotomous view." Others contend that man is composed of three parts—body, soul, and spirit (1 Thess. 5:23; Heb. 4:12). That would be the "trichotomous view." And others emphasize the wholeness of man; that is, that man is a whole person. That would be the "monochotomous view." The monochotomous view focuses on the use of the word "soul" to describe the whole person rather than just a part of man. As I stated, I believe that all three views are presented in Scripture and that specific descriptions are helpful in differing applications. Combining the soul (mind, emotions, and will) and spirit yields the immaterial part of man (see the appendix).

In the book of Galatians, Paul, discussing the battle between the flesh and the spirit, said, "Walk by the Spirit, and you will not carry out the desire of the flesh. For the flesh sets its desire against the Spirit, and the Spirit against the flesh; for these are in opposition to one another, so that you may not do the things that you please" (Gal. 5:16–17). In terms of the makeup of man, Paul here was portraying a combination of the body and soul, stating that both can be the source of the production of sinful activities. He continued: "Now the deeds of the flesh are evident ... envying [which is an emotion, found in the soul], drunkenness [which is physical, found in the body] ..." (Gal. 5:19–21). Thus, the body and soul combination yields the flesh.

The Make-Up of Man
Flesh and Spirit

The Battle of the Flesh and the Spirit

The following diagram shows the two parts of man: flesh and spirit. The center of the diagram is white, which is intended to show that this man is a Christian and has the Holy Spirit in him. However, the man has set his "will switch" (his chooser) on his flesh, and has thus chosen to live the flesh-led life.[36]

The *Flesh-Controlled* **Christian**

The "Will Switch"
Set on the Flesh

One of the most prominent stories in Scripture about the battle of the flesh and the spirit is that of Abraham and Sarah coming up with a plan to "help" God in His intention to give an heir to Abraham. They decided Abraham should go in to Hagar, Sarah's handmaiden, and take her as his wife. He did; and later she conceived and gave birth to Ishmael.

Abraham and Sarah experienced the negative results of living by the flesh as evidenced by the persecution of Isaac by his older brother (Gen. 21:9). The Lord had promised this difficulty with Ishmael (Gen. 16:12). Abraham and Sarah's one act of the flesh propelled into an adversarial relationship between the Jews and the Arabs that continues to this day.

Biblical records reveal many other instances in which people engaged in a battle between the flesh and the Spirit. The following individuals chose to embrace the flesh-led life:

Persons/Entities	Scripture Reference	Spiritual Battle
Adam, Eve, and the serpent	Genesis 3:1–7	Life, death, and the fruit of the Tree of the Knowledge of Good and Evil
Abraham, Sarah, and Hagar	Genesis 16:1–6	An heir
The Israelites and the Golden Calf	Exodus 32:1–6	Obedience to the Ten Commandments
The ten spies who voted not to go into the Promised Land while at Kadesh-Barnea	Numbers 13:25–33	Trusting God
Samson and Delilah	Judges 16:4–22	Concealing the source of Samson's strength
David, Bathsheba, and Uriah	2 Samuel 11–12	Adultery and covering it up
Solomon and his many wives	1 Kings 11:1–13	Obedience to God
The apostle Peter and his three denials of Christ	Mark 14:66–72	Fear of losing his life

The next diagram also shows the two parts of man, flesh and spirit, but in this diagram the man has set his "will switch" on the spirit, and has thus chosen to embrace a spirit-filled life. Notice that the walls of his inner core are opened up so the Holy Spirit can flow throughout him.

The *Spirit-Filled* Christian

The "Will Switch" *Set on the Spirit*

In Hebrews 11, the "Faith Hall of Fame," the author lists the following individuals who chose to live the Spirit-filled life:

Persons/Entities	Scripture Reference	Spiritual Battle
Abel	Hebrews 11:4	What to sacrifice
Noah	Hebrews 11:7	Obedience when it had never rained before
Abraham	Hebrews 11:8, 17	Obedience when instructed to move to an unknown location and sacrifice his son
Moses' parents	Hebrews 11:23	Placing baby Moses in a basket in the river

All of the heroes in the "Faith Hall of Fame" chose to live by faith rather than by the flesh in each of the instances referred to in this list. They were "examples for us," and these instances were "written for our instruction."

Sin and the Law

In Galatians 5:19–21, Paul listed the works of the flesh as: "immorality, impurity, sensuality, idolatry, sorcery, enmities, strife, jealousy, outbursts of anger, disputes, dissensions, factions, envying, drunkenness, carousing, and things like these." In some translations (such as the NIV), the world "flesh" is translated as "sinful nature." This is unfortunate, because the flesh is not a "nature," and we do not have to obey our flesh. However, it does portray the negative image of deeds, that we don't want to come forth from ourselves.

In 1 Corinthians 15:56, Paul said, "the power of sin is the law." The law gives strength to sin? Hard to believe! Furthermore, in Romans 7:5, Paul said sinful passions are "aroused by the Law." From this, it would seem (in this context) that our motivation to do good is based on the Mosaic law, or just "law," or Christian rules. However, obeying the Law can never make a person righteous, for "if righteousness comes through [obeying] the Law, then Christ died needlessly" (Gal. 2:21). Christianity is a relationship, not a religion; faith, not works; living by dependence on the Savior, not living by dependence on self.

Again, I will mention here a difference between the sons of Israel in the book of Exodus and the children of God who have received Jesus Christ as their Savior. Biblical historians refer to the period from Exodus to the cross as "the time of the Law" and the period from the cross through today as "the time of grace" (and also "the Church Age").[37] Christians no longer live under the Law, but under grace (Rom. 6:14). Ours is not a religion served by obeying certain rules, but a relationship with God the Father.

The Good News

In Exodus 17:14, we read, "Then the LORD said to Moses, 'Write this in a book as a memorial and recite it to Joshua, that I will utterly blot out the memory of Amalek from under heaven.'" The good news is that the battle with the flesh will have an end. However, while we are still here on earth, we must do our part in the battle—to trust in Jesus, live by faith, and lead the Spirit-filled life.

Moving Toward Milk and Honey

There is a spiritual war going on in this world and in your life. The Milk and Honey Man will have to engage in the battle of the flesh and the spirit until the end. When you recognize that fact and start trying to overcome the demands of the flesh by faith, you will have passed another milestone in your journey.

Chapter 12

The Mosaic Covenant

Lordship for the Milk and Honey Man

Exodus 19:1–8

OUR STORY IS about the pilgrimage of a Christian in pursuit of the victorious life. This life is available to all Christians, but arrived at by only a few. In terms of the Egypt-to-Canaan pilgrimage made by the sons of Israel, it is about the pursuit of the life of milk and honey. As Moses told the Israelites as they approached the Promised Land, the Lord "brought us into this place and has given us this land, a land flowing with milk and honey" (Deut. 26:9). Reaching the Promised Land was their goal.

How did the sons of Israel get to the land of milk and honey? And how do we get there? The journey, the pilgrimage, is key to the Christian life. It is the way of sanctification. It begins when we realize we are in bondage to sin and need God in our lives to free us from that bondage. It continues when we, like the Israelites at the time of the first Passover, apply the blood of the Lamb as our substitute. We also experience the death of our old self and accept the salvation from sin that Christ offers. The Israelites told the story of the Passover over and over for hundreds of years, and when the blood of the Lamb of God is applied in our lives, we are also impacted forever. We too have a story to tell.

In the Old Testament story of the Exodus, the Israelites witnessed the presence of God in the pillar of cloud and were "baptized" (identified) with Moses in the cloud and in the sea. As they stood on the east bank of the Red Sea, they could look at the drowning soldiers of the Egyptian army and be assured of their deliverance. They could also see the path of water across the

Red Sea close up, thus preventing their return to Egypt across the Red Sea. In that sequence of events, Christians learn about God's abiding presence, baptism, and assurance of salvation.

As the Israelites headed toward the Promised Land, they celebrated their deliverance from bondage, learned about handling bitterness, discovered they could rely upon God for food and water, and battled with the enemy. But the sons of Israel wouldn't really begin their new lives until they reached the Promised Land, and to reach that final destination, they had to be completely committed to the Lord. So let's take a closer look at total commitment as it relates to Israel since their journey is a type for us to follow in our own pilgrimage.

Covenants

God has given His people several covenants over time. For instance, after the great flood, when Noah and his family disembarked from the ark, God promised them, "I establish my covenant with you; and all flesh shall never again be cut off by the water of the flood, neither shall there again be a flood to destroy the earth" (Gen. 9:11). As a sign of this covenant, God set the rainbow in the sky. It would be used as a reminder of His commitment to His people.

God established a major covenant between Himself and Abraham, later known as the Father of the Jews (Gen. 12:1–3). In this well-known agreement known as the Abrahamic Covenant, God promised He would give Abraham land (the Promised Land), seed (descendants), and blessing. The promise of descendants was of special significance to Abraham and Sarah at that time because they were quite elderly and had no children. The promise was unilateral, one-sided: only God entered into the covenant. In fact, Abraham was asleep when God ratified the covenant. It was also unconditional; the sons of Israel did not have to do anything to reap the rewards that God had promised them. Furthermore, it was eternal in duration.

The Abrahamic Covenant had three corresponding branches (or "sub-covenants"): (1) the Palestinian Covenant of Deuteronomy 30:1–10, which was the covenant for the promise of land; (2) the Davidic Covenant of 2 Samuel 7:12–16, which was the covenant for the promise of seed (descendants); and (3) the New Covenant in Jeremiah 31:31–34, which was for the blessing and which is referred to by Jesus at the Last Supper (Luke 22:20).

The Mosaic Covenant

When the Israelites set out from Rephidim, they entered the Desert of Sinai and camped there in front of the mountain. At this point in their pilgrimage, God gave them another covenant (known as the Mosaic Covenant). Unlike the Abrahamic Covenant, there were two parties in this agreement: God and the sons of Israel. Not only did the Israelites have to participate in the agreement, but they also had to participate in the activity required by the agreement: obedience to God.

When Moses went up Mount Sinai to meet with God, the Lord said to him, "Thus you shall say to the house of Jacob and tell the sons of Israel: 'You yourselves have seen what I did to the Egyptians, and how I bore you on eagles' wings, and brought you to Myself. Now then, if you will indeed obey My voice and keep My covenant, then you shall be My own possession among all the peoples … and you shall be to Me a kingdom of priests and a holy nation'" (Ex. 19:3–6). The first part of Exodus 19:5 contains the condition of the agreement: "Now then, if you will indeed obey My voice and keep My covenant …" The Israelites were required to obey God.

It should be noted that the promises of land in the Mosaic Covenant had a conditional clause: "The LORD your God will prosper you abundantly … if you obey the LORD your God to keep His commandments" (Deut. 30:9–10). Although the Abrahamic Covenant was unconditional (the nation would get the land), the generation that would occupy it was conditional. Any given generation could be kept out of the land (as the first generation of the sons of Israel were) or kicked out of the land if they disobeyed the Lord. And we see the latter occurring in the history of the nation of Israel on three separate occasions: (1) when the northern ten tribes fell to Assyria in 722 BC, (2) when Judah fell to Babylon in 605–586 BC, and (3) during the Diaspora in AD 70. From this, we see that the Israelites' occupation of the land was contingent on their obedience.

The rewards for this obedience that God promised the sons of Israel in the Mosaic Covenant were that they would be God's own possession among all people and that they would be to Him a kingdom of priests and a holy nation (Ex. 19:5–6). The sons of Israel would belong to God—they would be His chosen people (Deut. 7:6; 14:2) and His representatives on earth—and when they arrived in the Promised Land, they were recognized as such. The occupants had heard about all that He had done for them.

Because God considered the Israelites His own people, they were shown a certain amount of favoritism. For instance, during the ten plagues in Egypt,

God made a distinction between the Israelites and the Egyptians. While the Egyptians suffered the effects of the plagues, the consequences of the plague did not apply to the Israelites. The sons of Israel did not receive the judgment that fell on the citizens of Egypt but instead received God's mercy. Being a child of God brought along with it the benefit of mercy.

Again, when the Israelites arrived in the Promised Land, the residents of that area not only knew that the Israelites belonged to Jehovah-God but also knew the reputation of how powerful God was and how He had delivered them. The people of Jericho, in particular, feared the sons of Israel.

The Israelites also were priests. Initially, Moses filled the role of intercessor, but later the sons of Israel had their own priesthood who interceded with the Lord on their behalf and who taught the Law to them. But they were also to be a kingdom of priests and serve those functions on a broader scale.

Finally, they were to be holy. Being obedient to God's Word was an indication of that holiness.

The Commitment

The covenant required a response to God's offer, so the Israelites committed to obey. At the time, they did not have any idea of the scope of what it would mean to obey the Lord, yet they committed to do so nonetheless. They said, "All that the LORD has spoken we will do" (Ex. 19:8)!

The sons of Israel had gone from making bricks under the Egyptian taskmasters to freedom—deliverance from their harsh bondage. They had received a leader, Moses, who was a child of Pharaoh's daughter and yet chose to be one with those of his own bloodline. They had seen the power of God and experienced His favoritism, as the harsh plagues did not harm them. They had walked through the waters of the Red Sea and had continued to experience the Lord for another three months as they made their way to the foot of Mount Sinai. So they knew God and made their commitment to obey the Law of Moses, even though they had no idea of the scope of that law. Because they had experienced God's deliverance, they chose to make a total commitment to the Mosaic Covenant.

Once the sons of Israel had made this pledge, Moses went up on the mountain to receive the Ten Commandments, and after this, they received even more instructions from God on how to live (Ex. 20–23). Now they had rules, knew what was expected, and could make an intelligent assessment of the proposed commitment. When the Israelites received these commandments, they repeated their commitment: "All the words which the LORD has spoken we will do" (Ex. 24:3). This was a Lordship commitment. This was a commitment to respond to Him as Lord of life. This was a time in Israel's history when there was a corporate acknowledgment of His Lordship—and a corporate statement of submission to it.

The Christian Commitment

It is common for a Christian to say to a non-Christian, "You need to trust Jesus and receive Him as your Savior and Lord." The combination of the terms "Savior and Lord" is found four times in the book of 2 Peter (1:11; 2:20; 3:2, and 3:18), and the statement tends to imply that the commitment to both aspects of Jesus Christ is simultaneous. However, while there is no doubt that some Christians receive Jesus as their Savior and as their Lord simultaneously, it seems that many do not. Some might accept the Savior part, but not the Lordship part. While they desire to take the benefits and blessings of forgiveness, they are not willing to relinquish their rights to be their own boss. Others simply don't see the two aspects at that point of salvation.

Jesus is the Savior of the world, and has been for all of time. But He is not your Savior until you place your trust in Him. Jesus is the Lord of life, but He is not your Lord until you commit to make Him so. Note that the Israelites did not commit to the Mosaic Covenant the same weekend they experienced the Passover. It was three months later. In the same way, it is appropriate to invite a person who has already experienced salvation to "present himself to Him" and submit to His Lordship.

Christians have no less of an obligation than the sons of Israel. Those who have learned Who the Lord is and realize He has delivered them from bondage to sin are exhorted to make Him the Lord of their lives. In Romans 12:1–2, Paul said we are to "present [our] bodies a living and holy sacrifice, acceptable to God, which is [our] spiritual service of worship. And do not be conformed to this world, but be transformed by the renewing of your mind, so that [we] may prove what the will of God is, that which is good and acceptable and perfect."

Please note that the burnt offering was wholly, entirely consumed. It symbolized the entire surrender to God of the individual or the congregation. The Romans 12:1 sacrifice is a total surrender.

This is a commitment to the Lordship of Jesus Christ. While we can certainly make a general commitment to do "all the words which the LORD has spoken," it is helpful to go through the list of things for which we naturally assume possession, and then give those things to the Lord. This could include material possessions such as a bank account, a house, a car, a boat, a TV, a DVR, a set of golf clubs, a hunting rifle, a dishwasher, a washer and dryer, a computer, an iPod, a cell phone, or even a Bible. These are tangible, visual objects. We should also surrender our right to use these things; for instance, our right to use the set of golf clubs for recreation purposes.

In addition, this list would also include the people with whom we are the closest in our lives: our spouse, our children, our grandchildren, our best friend, our pastor, our favorite teacher, or our children's teacher. If God were to move them to another place or take them home to be with Him today, we would be devastated. However, the loss would be easier to handle if we had given them to the Lord prior to their death. We must learn to live with the possibility that they could be removed from our lives at any time.

We are also called to give up ourselves—our minds, our will, our emotions, our health, our strength, our job, our integrity, our reputation, our resume, our values, our doctrinal beliefs, our right to be right, our right to be accepted, or our right to be a success. Sometimes it seems harder to give up the use of our mind, will, and emotion than the material possessions of life. However, there is more to surrendering to God than even these items: we must also give up our expectations. We must let go of our expectation to have a job (or even the right to have a job), an education, the credentials of a degree, the right to wear certain clothing, and even our future.

If you have not already consciously made this commitment to the Lord and are ready to do so now, you can pray the following prayer:

> Dear Lord, I give You permission to do anything You wish to me, with me, in me, or through me. I claimed the above items once as mine. Now they all belong to You and are under Your control. You can do with them anything You please. I willingly make this commitment in the Name and authority of the Lord Jesus Christ.[38]

_____   _____

Signed   Date

If that prayer is one you can pray, please do so. You might have previously functioned with Christ as Lord, but if you have never made it "official," I encourage you to do so.

Believers Are Chosen to Follow the Lord

Similar to the sons of Israel being "the chosen people," Christians are the "elect" people. The gospel of Mark records the following prophecy of Jesus: "Unless the Lord had shortened those days, no life would have been saved; but for the sake of the elect, whom He chose, He shortened the days" (Mark 13:20). A familiar passage on this same subject is found in Ephesians 1:4: "He chose us in Him before the foundation of the world." We are Christ's representatives. We are called by His name. We are Christians.

Like the sons of Israel, Jesus "has made us to be a kingdom, priests to His God and Father" (Rev. 1:6). We are to intercede for others and teach the Word of God to others. He has called us to be holy. He chose us that we "would be holy and blameless before Him" (Eph. 1:4). He "called us with a holy calling" (2 Tim. 1:9).

Think for a moment about why you are here. Why are you on this earth? What are you doing here? You are here to bring glory to God! You have purpose in life; a reason for your very existence. You are not just the product of some evolutionary process based on random mutations. No, you have been created by God and placed here on earth to accomplish His will. That is your purpose.

Map of the Pilgrimage

The following diagram is the third chronological "map" that compares the physical journey of the sons of Israel to those taking the pilgrimage of the Christian life in the twenty-first century. At this point, the Israelites have passed the milestones of bondage, the ten plagues, the pillar of cloud, the crossing of the Red Sea, the drowning of Pharaoh's army, the episode of the bitter water, the gift of manna from heaven, the provision of the water from the rock, and the battle with Amalek. They have now crossed the second threshold: the giving and accepting of the Mosaic Covenant at Mount Sinai.

The Israelites have not yet arrived in the land promised to them. They have not yet begun to live the life the Lord has planned for them. He never intended for them to spend their lives wandering in the wilderness. There will be more milestones ahead and another threshold for them to cross. These additional milestones will happen to the Israelites as examples for us, the New Testament believers.

CHRONOLOGICAL MAP
CROSSING THE SECOND THRESHOLD

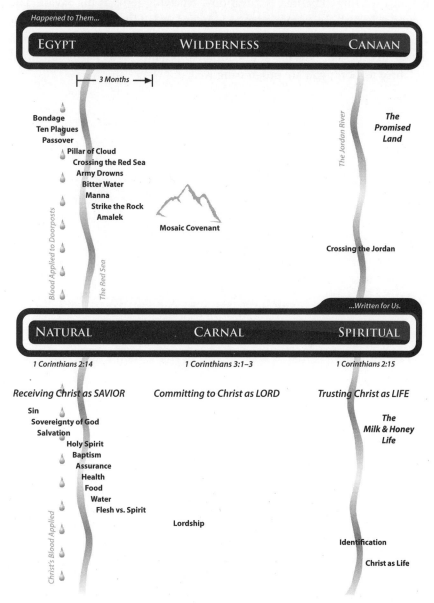

Happened to Them...

| EGYPT | WILDERNESS | CANAAN |

├── 3 Months ──┤

Bondage
Ten Plagues
Passover
Pillar of Cloud
Crossing the Red Sea
Army Drowns
Bitter Water
Manna
Strike the Rock
Amalek

Mosaic Covenant

The Jordan River

The Promised Land

Crossing the Jordan

Blood Applied to Doorposts

The Red Sea

...Written for Us.

| NATURAL | CARNAL | SPIRITUAL |

1 Corinthians 2:14   1 Corinthians 3:1–3   1 Corinthians 2:15

Receiving Christ as SAVIOR   Committing to Christ as LORD   Trusting Christ as LIFE

Sin
Sovereignty of God
Salvation
Holy Spirit
Baptism
Assurance
Health
Food
Water
Flesh vs. Spirit

Lordship

The Milk & Honey Life

Identification

Christ as Life

Christ's Blood Applied

97

Moving Toward Milk and Honey

As stated previously, the Milk and Honey Man has three thresholds to cross before he can experience the abundant kingdom life that God has planned for him. The first is salvation—receiving Jesus as his Savior. The second is Lordship—committing to Jesus as Lord of life. The third is Christ as Life, which is yet to come. Crossing all three thresholds is necessary for a person to experience the full abundant kingdom life. If you have committed to Christ as Lord, you are progressing well.

CHAPTER 13

The Mosaic Law

Grace for the Milk and Honey Man

EXODUS 20–23

AS WE SAW in the last chapter, the sons of Israel participated with the Lord in entering into a contract referred to as the "Mosaic Covenant." It was a bilateral agreement, thus both parties had to do their part to successfully consummate the deal. The Lord would not consider it a "done deal" until He had agreed that the Israelites had done their part. What, then, was their part?

As part of the agreement, the Lord provided the Israelites with certain rules and regulations that they had to follow. These were called the "Mosaic Law." The first group of these requirements were ten specific commands referred to as "the ten Commandments" (Ex. 20:1–17). The Lord presented these ten commandments to the Israelites right after they made their initial commitment to do all He had spoken (Ex. 19:8). These Ten Commandments were as follows:

1. "You shall have no other gods before Me" (Ex. 20:3).
2. "You shall not make for yourself an idol" (v. 4).
3. "You shall not take the name of the LORD your God in vain" (v. 7).
4. "Remember the Sabbath day, to keep it holy" (v. 8).
5. "Honor your father and your mother" (v. 12).
6. "You shall not murder" (v. 13).
7. "You shall not commit adultery" (v. 14).
8. "You shall not steal" (v. 15).
9. "You shall not bear false witness against your neighbor" (v. 16).
10. "You shall not covet" (v. 17).

In Exodus 20:22–26 and 21–23, the Lord gave the Israelites even more commandments. These commandments included laws about servants, capital offenses, physical injuries, animals, thieves, property damage, safekeeping of property and animals, borrowing, seduction of virgins, idolatry, care of the needy, justice, the Sabbath, and so forth. There were also other laws presented to the Israelites, which are listed elsewhere in the Pentateuch. These included moral laws, civil laws, and ceremonial laws (although they were not packaged into three books of the Bible). The sons of Israel were supposed to keep the Law—or, at least, to try to do so. Their obedience to the Law was intended to move them toward a righteous life.

Relationship of Christians to the Law

The following diagram depicts a timeline as it relates to God's dealings with people throughout history. The cross has been placed in the middle of the timeline to reflect the fact that all of history revolves around the birth, life, crucifixion, and resurrection of the Lord Jesus Christ. On the left side of the cross are the words "Old Testament" to indicate that the focus at that time was on the Jews as God's chosen people (and therefore His representatives). On the right side of the cross are the words "New Testament" to indicate that the focus has shifted to believers in Jesus Christ (both Jews and Gentiles, who are the representatives of God since the cross of Christ).

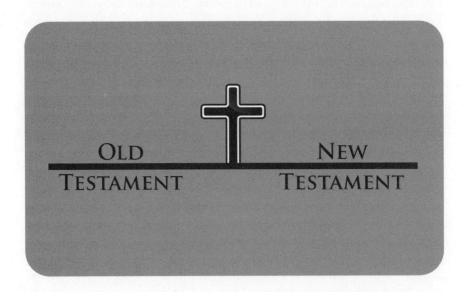

The next diagram reveals the primary operating principles of "law" and "grace" in terms of the time relationship between God and His people. Note that individuals were saved by grace through faith based on the blood of Jesus Christ in *every* generation. Nevertheless, the Law was dominant until Christ paid the penalty for humanity's sins on the cross. The animal sacrifices that were required to atone for sins (particularly the Day of Atonement) during the time of the Law had a temporary benefit in that they only lasted for one year. The blood of the lambs that were sacrificed pointed to Christ's payment, as the true Lamb of God, which had a permanent benefit in it that it was done once for all of time. Since then, Christ's followers have looked back to the cross in remembrance of what He has done.

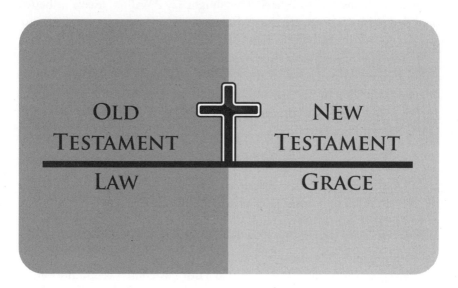

One of the places in Scripture where we find much about the Law is Psalm 119, which is the longest of the psalms (176 verses). It describes the Law in various terms: "testimonies," "precepts," "commandments," "statutes," "judgments," "ordinances," and "Your word." In my early Christian walk, I viewed these as references to specific rules that were to be obeyed. However, I now see that these describe a way of life—a way of life God encourages us to follow so we may lead fulfilling lives. Yet obedience to this Law could never provide a permanent solution to the problem of people's separation from God, as is seen in the fact that the Israelites had to repeat the ceremonies on the Day of Atonement every year. As Christians we don't have to do that, because Jesus paid our debt in full.

Jesus and the Law

Jesus said, "Do not think that I came to abolish the Law or the Prophets; I did not come to abolish but to fulfill" (Matt. 5:17). What was the purpose of the Mosaic Law? "The law came in so that the transgression would increase; but where sin increased, grace abounded all the more" (Rom. 5:20). The purpose of the Law is to enable people to see when they have not lived up to God's standards. When a Christian realizes he has violated God's instructions for holiness and righteousness, he confesses his sins and tries not to repeat the same act again. It is the Law that brings him to this realization.

Oftentimes, people will attempt to downplay the severity of their sins by comparing themselves to others. They might say, "Well, at least I'm better than that person." Scripture clearly points out that if a person commits just one sin, he has broken God's Law: "For whoever keeps the whole law and yet stumbles in one point, he has become guilty of all" (James 2:10). Imagine a ship secured by an anchor at the end of a long chain. In the same way it only takes one link in the chain to break for the ship to drift away from the anchor, it only takes the committing of one sin to break the Law to violate God's standard of perfection.

Furthermore, regarding the purpose of the Law, Paul told us, "the law has become our tutor to lead us to Christ, so that we may be justified by faith" (Gal. 3:24). The Law reveals we have a need and that a solution is required to fulfill that need. Jesus provided this solution when He took our place (became our substitute) and died on the cross to pay the penalty for our sin. We must exercise faith in Jesus Christ, and Him alone, to obtain this solution and consummate God's plan of salvation.

Paul goes on to say, "But now that faith has come, we are no longer under a tutor" (Gal. 3:25). When Christ came into the world and paid the penalty for our sin through His death on the cross, the Mosaic Law, as a rule of life for those who have faith in Christ, was terminated. Those who put their faith in Jesus Christ are no longer under the rule of the Mosaic law. As Paul wrote, "Sin shall not be master over you, for you are not under law but under grace" (Rom. 6:14).

Some Christians put up a "fence" to prevent violating their relationship with God. They draw a line to mark how far they can go before they cross the line of sinning against God. However, we should not be seeking to test the boundary of how far we can go without sinning. Rather, we should be trying to live to please God. Attempting to determine the boundary line for sinning is living by the Law.

In his letter to the Galatians, the apostle Paul has much to say about the importance of Christians living by faith rather than by self-effort (or "works of the Law"). The true gospel is by grace/faith/Spirit. In other words, a person is saved by grace through faith and receives the Spirit of God to enable and empower him to lead a life that is pleasing to God. As Christians, we are to live by the power the Holy Spirit (not self-effort), by faith (not works), and by God's grace (not some set of rules). Doing otherwise indicates we are living by the false gospel of law/works/flesh.

Circumcision

One of the issues in the early church was whether Gentiles were required to become circumcised when they came to Christ. This practice of circumcision, which began with Abraham in Genesis 17, was instituted by God to be a sign of the Israelites' covenant with Him. It was instituted before the Mosaic Law and became part of the law for the Israelites.

However, Paul said in Galatians that new believers are no longer required to be held to this practice. In Galatians 5:1, he wrote, "It was for freedom that Christ set us free; therefore keep standing firm and do not be subject again to a yoke of slavery." He went on to say, "If you receive circumcision, Christ will be of no benefit to you. I testify again to every man who receives circumcision, that he is under obligation to keep the whole law. You have been severed from Christ, you who are seeking to be justified by law; you have fallen from grace" (Gal. 5:2–4).

No Man is Justified by Law

If following the old Law, or any man-made set of rules, made us righteous or acceptable to God, we could then boast about our righteousness. But as Paul said, "Where then is boasting? It is excluded. By what kind of Law? Of works? No, but by a law of faith" (Rom. 3:27). No one can boast because the law of faith takes away the concept of righteousness by works and self-effort. We have been set free from living life by a set of rules. "The law of the Spirit of life in Christ Jesus has set [us] free from the law of sin and of death." (Rom. 8:2). That is freedom in Christ! We are no longer under a set of rules.

Of course, this does not mean we should stop trying to follow God's rules. If we love Jesus, we will naturally want to obey the guidelines for life found in the New Testament. We will want to love God, love our neighbor, love our wife, honor our father and mother, not get drunk, not be a glutton, not slander, not gossip, not steal, not commit adultery, not covet our neighbor's property. If we truly love Jesus, we won't want to do these things or a multitude of other things prohibited by the Law.

In Galatians 3:13, Paul wrote, "Christ redeemed us from the curse of the law, having become a curse for us—for it is written, 'CURSED IS EVERYONE WHO HANGS ON A TREE.'" Notice that Paul describes the requirement of living under the Law a "curse." However, we were relieved from that difficulty by the one who hung on the tree (cross) for us. Jesus took our place, and we are no longer under that curse.

The "power of sin is the law" (1 Cor. 15:56). If we are living by a law, a rule or a regulation, it has power over us. Our tendency will be to fight against it, because it is a law. No one likes to have a tyrant run his or her life. But every time we look to some rule or law as a requirement for life, we place our self under its power.

Melchizedek

The Law was not only a set of rules to live by but also a legal system. The system required a priest to intercede between God and the people. The people gave a sacrifice as a confession of their sins, and the priest killed the animal and sprinkled the blood. During the periods of the tabernacle and the temple, the blood was sprinkled on the mercy seat over the ark of the covenant. It was called the place of mercy because God saw the blood and was merciful.

Aaron was the first priest, the high priest, in the religious system set up by the Mosaic law. All priests thereafter were descendants of Aaron, and they all came from the tribe of Levi. Those of the tribe of Levi who were not priests were simply referred to as "Levites." The priests interceded, made the sacrifices, taught the Law, served as judges, and, in general, performed the religious rites for the people of Israel. The high priest held his position for life.

The diagram below again shows the timeline with the periods of Law and grace, but this time it also includes the priest for the period. Aaron, Moses' brother, was the first priest of the period of Law. He was the high priest and the father of all subsequent priests until Jesus. He was the originator of the Aaronic priesthood, and all subsequent priests were required to be descendants of his. The Aaronic priesthood taught the Law, interpreted the Law, and enforced the Law.

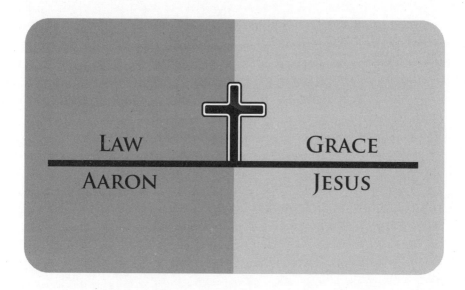

Aaron was from the tribe of Levi, and because of this the priesthood was sometimes referred to as the "Levitical priesthood." However, Jesus, the high priest of the time of grace, was from the tribe of Judah (He is referred to as "the Lion of Judah" in Rev. 5:5). We first read of Jesus being referred to as a priest in Psalm 110:4, where the psalmist wrote, "The LORD has sworn and will not change His mind, 'You are a priest forever according to the order of Melchizedek.'" This psalm was a prophecy of Jesus' assignment and revealed that His priesthood was to be of the order of Melchizedek, who lived before the institution of the Mosaic Law.

Melchizedek was the head of a priestly order known as the "order of Melchizedek." He first shows up in Genesis 14 after Abram delivered his nephew, Lot, from Chedorlaomer, the king of Elam, and the other kings who were with him. Melchizedek performed the priestly functions of blessing Abram, serving him communion, and receiving tithes from him. This was done before the Mosaic Law and the Levitical system had been instituted. In the diagram below, I have labeled this time as the period of "Pre-Law."

According to the book of Hebrews, there needed to be a change in the priesthood—a change from the Aaronic priesthood to a different form of priesthood. "Now if perfection was through the Levitical priesthood . . . what further need was there for another priest to arise according to the order of Melchizedek" (Heb. 7:11). The Levitical priests could not produce perfect people. What could? The Lord Jesus Christ! Jesus was a priest of another order, the order of Melchizedek. And, as the writer of Hebrew says, "When

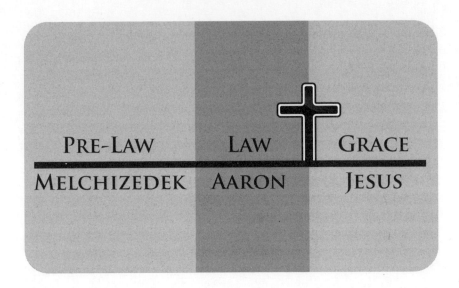

the priesthood is changed, of necessity there takes place a change of law also" (Heb. 7:12). Because Jesus came, we are no longer under law but are under grace.

Moving Toward Milk and Honey

We are free from the Law and no longer under it. We are to live by faith, not by keeping the Law. If you understand this—if it is real to you—then you have crossed another milestone toward becoming a Milk and Honey Man.

CHAPTER 14

The Golden Calf

Failure for the Milk and Honey Man

Exodus 32

THE FIRST COMMANDMENT the Israelites had promised to follow was, "You shall have no other gods before Me" (Ex. 20:3). God had shown the false gods of Egypt to be impotent, and He did not want the Israelites to worship anything but the living Lord.

The second commandment was, "You shall not make for yourself an idol, or any likeness of what is in heaven above or on the earth beneath or in the water under the earth. You shall not worship them or serve them; for I, the Lord your God, am a jealous God" (Ex. 20:4–5). This meant that the sons of Israel were to create no statues, no paintings, no figurines—nothing! They were to worship the Lord God, not an idol or image.

The third commandment the sons of Israel promised to follow was, "You shall not take the name of the Lord your God in vain, for the Lord will not leave him unpunished who takes His name in vain" (Ex. 20:7). The Israelites made vain, empty, and hollow promises to God when they agreed to follow His commands and then immediately violated the first two. Their promises were worthless and had no value or significance.

A Long Absence

Once the sons of Israel had agreed to the terms of the covenant, the Lord told Moses to get the people ready, for He was going to come down on Mount Sinai in the sight of all the people. "So it came about on the third day, when it was morning, that there were thunder and lightning flashes and a thick cloud upon the mountain and a very loud trumpet sound, so that all the people who were in the camp trembled" (Ex. 19:16–17).

When the people saw the presence of God, they trembled in fear. But Moses said to them, "Do not be afraid; for God has come in order to test you, and in order that the fear of Him may remain with you, so that you may not sin" (Ex. 20:20). After this, Moses went up the mountain to talk with the Lord, and he stayed up there long enough for the Israelites to forget (or, actually, to minimize) the things the Lord had done for them through Moses. Despite all the sons of Israel had witnessed on their journey, and despite the warnings they had received about violating the terms of the covenant, the Israelites ignored the Lord's instructions to them—particularly His prohibition of worshiping false gods.

As we read in Exodus 32:1, "When the people saw that Moses delayed to come down from the mountain, the people assembled about Aaron and said to him, 'Come, make us a god who will go before us; as for this Moses, the man who brought us up from the land of Egypt, we do not know what has become of him.'" In direct opposition to the command of the Lord, the Israelites asked Moses' brother to make an idol. And this was only approximately a month after they had received the commandment to make no idols and had committed to obey the commandments.

So the people surrendered their gold earrings, and Aaron shaped the gold into a calf. We read of idols of wood and stone, but this was an idol of molded metal. Then Aaron said, "Tomorrow shall be a feast to the Lord" (Ex. 32:5). However, this was not to be a feast to the Lord, the One true God, but to a false god that could neither hear nor speak. This golden calf could well be a representation of the Egyptian false god Apis, which was thought to be behind the success of the Egyptian economy (whenever this "god" was being favorable). As we have seen, the Lord had already defeated this false god with pestilence on the Egyptian cows (the fifth plague), and He also made provision for the Israelites with food from heaven (manna) and water from the rock. In this way, He had doubly defeated this false god. Therefore, the golden calf event made God extremely angry. Worship of an idol is worship of a false god, for an idol is no god at all. "So the next day they rose early and offered burnt offerings and brought peace offerings; and the people sat down to eat and to drink, and rose up to play" (Ex. 32:6). They had an orgy!

The Israelites disobeyed God, and the Lord was not pleased. "Then the LORD spoke to Moses, 'Go down at once, for your people, whom you brought up from the land of Egypt, have corrupted themselves'" (Ex. 32:7). He then told Moses to leave Him, for He was about to destroy the people and make Moses into a great nation (Ex. 32:10). But when Moses interceded on behalf of the people, the Lord relented.

Of course, this did not mean the people did not suffer consequences for their sin. When Moses returned to the camp, He said to the people, "Whoever is for the LORD, come to me!" (Ex. 32:26). The sons of Levi gathered to him, and together they drew their swords and went through the camp, killing the revelers. About 3,000 of the people died that day. Forty years later, when the children and grandchildren of these Israelites were about to enter the Promised Land, Moses would remind them of the great sin the people had committed on that day (Deut. 9:12–14).

The New Testament records this incident as one of the things that "took place as examples for us, that we might not desire evil as they did" (1 Cor. 10:6). We are warned to learn from this bad example: "Do not be idolaters as some of them were; as it is written, 'The people sat down to eat and drink and rose up to play'" (1 Cor. 10:7).

For the Israelites, this represented a failure. A big-time failure!

Moving Toward Milk and Honey

When Moses went up Mount Sinai and was absent from the camp for a long period of time, certain instigators among the people convinced Aaron to make a golden calf and thus led the sons of Israel astray. This was not the way to worship the Lord. It was not the path to milk and honey. In your life, you must learn the proper subject of true worship, and then worship Him in spirit and in truth (John 4:24). When you do, you have set your table for Milk and Honey. You will have also passed another milestone—the milestone of failure, recognition of failure, repentance from failure, and restoration to the pursuit of the Lord and His ways.

CHAPTER 15

Failure at Kadesh-Barnea

Rejection of Living by Faith

NUMBERS 13:17–33

AFTER THE SONS of Israel had spent a year-and-a-half in the wilderness, they came to Kadesh-Barnea, where they sent out twelve spies, one from each tribe, to spy out the land and its inhabitants. Moses told them,

> Go up there into the Negev; then go up into the hill country. See what the land is like, and whether the people who live in it are strong or weak, whether they are few or many. How is the land in which they live, is it good or bad? And how are the cities in which they live, are they like open camps or with fortifications? How is the land, is it fat or lean? Are there trees in it or not?
>
> —Num. 13:17–20

The twelve spied out the land and came back at the end of forty days with this report: "We went in to the land where you sent us; and it certainly does flow with milk and honey, and this is its fruit" (Num. 13:27). However, though the spies gave a good report on the land, they gave a bad report on the Israelites' chances of conquering it: "Nevertheless, the people who live in the land are strong, and the cities are fortified and very large; and moreover, we saw the descendants of Anak there. Amalek is living in the land of the Negev and the Hittites and the Jebusites and the Amorites are living in the hill country, and the Canaanites are living by the sea and by the side of the Jordan" (Num. 13:28–29). In other words, the spies were saying, "Even though the land is great, the people are too big, too strong, and too many for us to conquer it."

110

At that moment, Caleb, representing the tribe of Judah, spoke up and said to the people, "We should by all means go up and take possession of it, for we will surely overcome it" (Num. 13:30). It had only been eighteen months since the Lord had performed ten mighty miracles to demonstrate His superior capability to that of the Egyptian false gods. Even the residents of Jericho knew about the Israelites being delivered across the Red Sea (Josh. 2:10). So did Caleb. He remembered the ten plagues and how the Lord had delivered the entire nation across the Red Sea on dry land. He remembered the various manifestations of God's hand on the way to Mt. Sinai and when the Israelites were camped there. This is why he could be so confident and so bold at this moment. The rest of the people should have been bold, too, but they were not.

So the controversy was stirred up.

> But the men who had gone up with him said, "We are not able to go up against the people, for they are too strong for us." So they gave out to the sons of Israel a bad report of the land which they had spied out, saying, "The land through which we have gone, in spying it out, is a land that devours its inhabitants; and all the people whom we saw in it are men of great size. ... and we became like grasshoppers in our own sight, and so we were in their sight."
>
> —Num. 13:31–33

The spies' lack of faith caused them to look down on themselves and question the Israelites' ability to take possession of the land that God promised them. At this point, the spies and the people thought that those residing in the land were superior to them and that the Israelites were not up to the task of the invasion. So the congregation of the sons of Israel began to weep and complain to Moses and Aaron that it would have been better for them if they had died in the land of Egypt or in the wilderness (Num. 14:2). They even began to consider appointing a new leader who would take them back to Egypt (Num. 14:3–4).

Then Joshua and Caleb spoke to the Israelites, saying, "The land which we passed through to spy out is an exceedingly good land. If the LORD is pleased with us, then He will bring us into this land and give it to us—a land which flows with milk and honey. Only do not rebel against the Lord; and do not fear the people of the land, for they will be our prey. Their protection has been removed from them, and the Lord is with us; do not fear them" (Num. 14:7–9). Unfortunately, the congregation was not persuaded by these words and the tribes of Israel did not think God could or would bring them into the land or that He would give them the victory. They did not have faith.

A Type of the Milk and Honey Man

Caleb bar Jephunneh (that is, Caleb the son of Jephunneh) was an Old Testament Milk and Honey Man. He might have looked forward to the material blessings he would receive when he lived in the Promised Land, but he also desired to be where God wanted the sons of Israel to be. He submitted to the Lord's will and trusted God in every endeavor. Because of his faith, the Lord told Moses, "My servant Caleb, because he has had a different spirit and has followed Me fully, I will bring him into the land which he entered, and his descendants shall take possession of it" (Num. 14:24).

Later, David, who was also from the tribe of Judah, proved to be another man who had a different spirit and lived by faith. When the Philistine giant, Goliath, challenged the army of Israel, David volunteered to take him on. When they met, David said,

> You come to me with a sword, a spear, and a Javelin, but I come to you in the name of the LORD of hosts, the God of the armies of Israel, whom you have taunted. This day the LORD will deliver you up into my hands, and I will strike you down and remove your head from you … that all the earth may know that there is a God in Israel, and that all this assembly may know that the LORD does not deliver by sword or by spear; for the battle is the LORD's and He will give you into our hands.
>
> —1 Sam. 17:45–46

David was called a man after God's own heart. He trusted God!

Centuries after this, the Lord Jesus Christ was born of the tribe of Judah. He trusted and obeyed His heavenly Father. When facing crucifixion, He prayed, "Father, if you are willing, remove this cup from Me; yet not My will, but Yours, be done" (Luke 22:42). Our Savior lived and died by faith.

A Christian hymn proclaims, "Trust and obey, for there's no other way, to be happy in Jesus, but to trust and obey."[39] Those two words are like two sides of a coin. If you trust God, you can easily obey Him. If you obey God, it is because you know He is trustworthy and that you can trust Him. If you are a Milk and Honey Man, you rest in God's direction and His provision.

Judgment at Kadesh-Barnea

After Caleb and Joshua made their plea to their fellow Israelites to follow the Lord and go forward into the Promised Land, the congregation wanted to stone them (Num. 14:10). The Lord was angry with the people's rebellion and said to Moses, "How long will this people spurn Me? And how long will they not believe in Me, despite all the signs which I have performed in their midst?" (v. 11). Then the Lord again threatened to destroy the Israelites and make a new nation out of Moses. But Moses once more interceded and made a plea to the Lord to pardon the sin of the sons of Israel, and God did (v. 20).

Before pronouncing judgment on the Israelites, the Lord said the sons of Israel "have seen My glory and My signs which I performed in Egypt and in the wilderness, yet have put Me to the test these ten times and have not listened to My voice" (v. 22). The sons of Israel had repeatedly tested God. Their lack of faith was the issue. So God pronounced His judgment: "Your corpses will fall in this wilderness, even all your numbered men, according to your complete number from twenty years old and upward, who have grumbled against Me. Surely you shall not come into the land in which I swore to settle you" (vv. 29–30). Only Caleb and Joshua were exempted from this judgment.

Previously, we examined how the covenant with Abraham for land, seed, and blessings was a unilateral covenant. The land had been given to the Israelites. However, only those generations who were obedient to the Lord were allowed to occupy the land. This generation had demonstrated that they were unwilling to depend on the Lord to take them into the land, so they were not allowed to go in and possess it.

The Lord's judgment at Kadesh-Barnea included a time element: "Your sons shall be shepherds for forty years in the wilderness, and will suffer for your unfaithfulness, until your corpses lie in the wilderness" (Num. 14:33). Up to this point, the sons of Israel had been travelling about eighteen months since the time they crossed the Red Sea.[40] This means they would be left to wander in the wilderness for thirty-eight and a half years.

The generation who had been delivered from Egypt had not learned Who God was and how trustworthy He is. The starting point for Israel's new life would be the Promised Land, but it would begin with a generation who would trust God and follow Him in faith.

An Example for Us

The sons of Israel hardened their hearts against God and did not trust Him. They tested God, and as a result God did not allow them to enter into His rest (Heb. 3:8–10). The sons of Israel experienced real trials and physical hardships. These were disciplines for them, but their hardships were for our instruction.

Like the Israelites, Christians can be disobedient to the Lord's instructions and be disciplined for the purpose of correction. This discipline proves God's love, and afterward it yields the peaceful fruit of righteousness (Heb. 12:6, 11.) Arriving at the Promised Land was not the end of life; it was the beginning. Canaan was not a type of heaven; it is a type of the abundant life, the Christ-led life, the Spirit-filled life.

Hebrews 3:7–4:11 is an important section of Scripture in terms of our learning how to live based on the experiences of the sons of Israel. This is one of five warning passages for Christians contained in the book of Hebrews. It is an admonishment to Christians to learn from the lesson of Israel's failures in the wilderness.

In Hebrews 3:12, the author warned, "See to it, brothers, that none of you has a sinful, unbelieving heart that turns away from the living God" (NIV). The writer went on to say, "So we see that they were not able to enter [the Promised Land], because of unbelief" (v. 19). In each of these verses, the author precedes the Greek root word *pistos* (which means faith, trust, or belief) by the negative article *a*. For this reason, some people believe the author is referring to non-believers, as in the "unsaved."[41] However, the sons of Israel who applied the blood to the two doorposts and the lintel were redeemed people. In the book of Exodus, the Lord promised to redeem the sons of Israel before they left Egypt (Ex. 6:6) and referred to them as a redeemed people in Exodus 15:13. A person can conduct life without trusting the Lord—that is, without living by faith—and yet believe in Christ's saving grace for eternity.

The unbelieving aspect of the Israelites at Kadesh-Barnea was their lack of trust in God's ability to bring them into the Promised Land. As we have discussed, their numerous past experiences proved that He could and would meet their needs of the moment, and therefore they should have trusted Him going forward. Their ancestor, Abraham, "the Father of the Jews," had left Ur of the Chaldeans (Gen. 11:31) and followed God by faith, and the Israelites in the wilderness should have done the same.

Modern-day Experiences of Failure and Brokenness

All of us fail. Even those who are sold out to Him will fail. We will fail in our obedience—in our attempts to be holy people. We will fail in our service—in our attempts to glorify Him. It happens to pastors, teachers, Christian counselors, elders, deacons, missionaries, Sunday School teachers, new Christians and long-time Christians, young ones and old ones, and other committed Christians.

The sons of Israel failed because they refused to trust God and enter the Promised Land. This was an exercise of their flesh. Likewise, the following testimonies report the failures of several men of God who did not recognize they were conducting ministry by the power of their flesh. They did not conduct ministry by the power of God and enter into the "rest" of the Lord by trusting Him.

Major Ian Thomas

Ian Thomas was taken to church as a child, led to salvation at a Crusaders Union Camp at age twelve, and began to do open air preaching when he was fifteen. About that time he committed to becoming a foreign missionary. He was so committed that his life was constant activity. He decided that the best way he could serve the Lord was to become a doctor. This would require the preparation of college studies.

In the introduction to Major Ian Thomas's book *The Saving Life of Christ*, Dr. V. Raymond Edman, past president of Wheaton College, wrote about the following experience of Ian Thomas:

> At the university Ian became a leader in the Inter-Varsity Fellowship group. If ever there was any evangelistic activity going on, this youthful zealot was "buzzing around the place, every holiday, every spare moment!" He started a slum club down in the East End of London. "Out of a sheer desire to win souls, to go out and get them, I was a windmill of activity until, at the age of nineteen, every moment of my day was packed tight with doing things. ... Thus by the age of nineteen, I had been reduced to a state of complete exhaustion spiritually, until I felt that there was no point in going on. ...
>
> "Then, one night in November, that year, just at midnight ... I got down on my knees before God, and I just wept in sheer despair. I said, 'Oh, God, I know that I am saved. I love Jesus Christ. I am perfectly convinced that I am converted. With all my heart I have wanted to serve

Thee. I have tried to my uttermost and I am a hopeless failure!'" ... That night things happened.

"I can honestly say that I had never once heard from the lips of men the message that came to me then ... but God that night simply focused upon me the Bible message of Christ Who is our life. ... The Lord seemed to make plain to me that night, through tears of bitterness: 'You see, for seven years, with utmost sincerity, you have been trying to live for Me, on My behalf, the life that I have been waiting for seven years to live through you.'

That night, all in the space of an hour, Ian Thomas discovered the secret of the adventurous life. He said, "I got up the next morning to an entirely different Christian life, but I want to emphasize this: I had not received one iota more than I already had for seven years!"

Thus step by step the Most High led His trusting and obedient servant into paths that he neither foresaw nor chose, but they were pathways of service eminently satisfying and always adventurous. Instead of medical school and the mission field, the ministry was evangelism throughout Britain, especially among young people.[42]

Steve McVey

Steve McVey had been a very successful pastor in Alabama as measured by man. He had the most baptisms at his church, a growing attendance, successful programs, and love and affirmation from his congregation. The Jaycees had recognized him as an "outstanding young religious leader." Then he moved to pastor a church in Atlanta, and after a year of the same effort, nothing happened in his new church. By his own standards, he was a failure. For the first time in seventeen years, a church he had pastored had declined in attendance. He had failed miserably.

Steve writes in his book *Grace Walk*,

It was at 1:00 AM on October 6, 1990, that I lay on my face in my office, crying. The previous year had brought me to a place of absolute brokenness. I had prayed for God to make me stronger, but He had a different plan. He was making me weaker. So there I lay, broken and hopeless. In seventeen hours I would have to stand in my pulpit on Sunday evening and deliver a "State of the Church Address." Either I could build a straw man of success or I could tell the truth. I didn't have the strength to pretend or the courage to be honest, so I prayed and cried. When I finished, I prayed and cried some more.[43]

Bob George

Bob George, founder of Discipleship Counseling Services in Dallas and host of the radio talk show *People to People*, was converted to Christianity as a businessman and went into vocational ministry. Then he burned out on "religion." He reported his continuing effort to serve the Lord in his book *Classic Christianity*: "I still taught Bible studies. I still shared my faith. But it became more of a performance. Instead of doing it because I wanted to, I did it because I was expected to do it. I was reminded to have a daily quiet time. I had to fill out reports indicating how many people I shared Christ with and how many Bible studies I was leading. My joy ebbed away."[44]

Moving Toward Milk and Honey

For God to use us, we have to be sold out to Him. We have to be delivered from our own self-capability and come to the realization that all our energy is wasted apart from the breaking that comes with deliverance from self to full trust in God. The sons of Israel had to get that same message, and forty years was a lengthy education. When you recognize the utter incapability of self and are broken of it, you can record a major milestone in your journey toward becoming a Milk and Honey Man.

CHAPTER 16

Speak to the Rock
Only One Crucifixion
NUMBERS 20:2–13

AFTER THE ISRAELITES' failure at Kadesh-Barnea, the Lord led His people to a place with a drinking water problem for the third time. As you will recall, the first incident, which occurred at the village of Marah, was a trial with bitter water. When God instructed Moses to throw a tree into the waters, the bitterness was eliminated and the Lord was revealed as the Healer of diseases (Ex. 15:22–26).

The second trial occurred at Rephidim when the Lord instructed Moses to strike a rock with his staff and water poured out (Ex. 17:1–7). For the second time the sons of Israel received proof that the Lord could and would provide.

The third occasion, recorded in this chapter of the book of Numbers, represented another bump in the road for the sons of Israel. The Israelite community had arrived at the Desert of Zin, and once again there was no water for the people to drink. This would represent another trial, another lesson from God.

Water from the Rock

The people assembled themselves against Moses and Aaron and began to complain. "Why have you made us come up from Egypt, to bring us in to this wretched place? It is not a place of grain or figs or vines or pomegranates, nor is there water to drink" (Num. 20:5). So Moses and Aaron went to the tent of meeting and talked to the Lord. The Lord told Moses, "Take the rod; and you and your brother Aaron assemble the congregation and speak to the rock before their eyes, that it may yield its water" (v. 8).

Moses and Aaron did as the Lord asked and gathered the sons of Israel before the rock. Then he said to them, "Listen now, you rebels; shall we bring forth water for you out of this rock?" (v. 10). After this, Moses lifted up his hand and struck the rock twice with his rod. Water came out, and the people and their beasts began to drink (vv. 10–11). Notice that Moses spoke to the people, but not to the rock as God had instructed.

I was recently exposed to some teaching on this passage that claimed Moses first spoke to the rock, waited, then struck the rock, waited again, and then struck the rock a second time. To me, that would seem like impatience. As I have reread this passage, I am convinced that Moses was angry with the people and that he struck the rock out of his anger, not his impatience.

Regardless, the point is the same: Moses was disobedient (Num. 27:14 NIV). And there would be consequences for this disobedience: "The LORD said to Moses and Aaron, 'Because you have not believed Me, to treat Me as holy in the sight of the sons of Israel, therefore you shall not bring this assembly into the land which I have given them'" (Num. 20:12). Neither Moses or Aaron would enter the Promised Land.

A Break in the Type

Ironically, we never read of any punishment that Moses received for killing a man back in Egypt. However, here we see him punished for his disobedience in striking the rock. Why? Because this disobedience was important to God.

Types are resemblances planned by God. A particular type in the Old Testament was designed in such a way that it carried a likeness to the antitype in the New Testament. Likewise, the antitype was planned by God to be the fulfillment and heightening of the type. Because centuries of time separated most of the types from their antitypes, they obviously required God's planning to have the types depict or picture the antitypes.

As Dr. Roy B. Zuck notes in *Basic Bible Interpretation,* "This fact shows that types have apologetic value, for typology points to the evidence of divine design between the Old and New Testaments."[45] The complementary aspect of typology from numerous different writers from different walks of life also is evidence of the divine design.

The sovereignty of God is demonstrated in typology. However, lest we think we are all just robots, note that Moses was given the freedom to disobey. In this case, the New Testament indicates that the rock was a type of Christ (1 Cor. 10:4). To speak to the rock would thus mean to pray. God had intended to use this as a lesson on prayer, but instead Moses struck the rock twice. Striking the rock was a type of the crucifixion of Christ. Striking it twice would have suggested that Jesus could be, and for some purpose needed to be, crucified a second time. But Jesus was dead after the first crucifixion, and His first and only crucifixion paid the whole penalty for our sins (Heb. 7:27; 10:10).

In his disobedience (Num. 27:14 NIV), Moses broke the type that God wanted to set up. That is why Moses' obedience in this instance was so important. It also reveals the importance for us to obey God, even when we don't understand His reasons.

Moving Toward Milk and Honey

God wanted to teach the Israelites a lesson about prayer, but this time, due to Moses' anger, they could not learn from the incident. This reminds us that we have a sovereign Creator who predetermined each of these lessons in the Old Testament as an example for us and that we have the freedom to obey or disobey His commands. We also learn that we, too, must be obedient. When you grasp these concepts, you've passed another milestone in becoming a Milk and Honey Man.

CHAPTER 17

The Bronze Serpent

Jesus Lifted Up

NUMBERS 21:4–9

AS WE OBSERVED earlier, when the Lord began to lead the sons of Israel to the Promised Land, they did not take the shortest route. This was deliberate on His part. He had lessons for them to learn so that they could be "My own possession among all the peoples, for all the earth is mine" and "a kingdom of priests and a holy nation" (Ex. 19:5–6).

After the Israelites, while at Kadesh-Barnea, had shown that they were unwilling to trust the Lord to enable them to enter into the Promised Land, the Lord passed judgment on them and told them that they would spend an additional forty years in the wilderness. Many of the lessons they would learn after the event at Kadesh-Barnea were for the purpose of discipline, while others were for the purpose of re-educating them regarding God's way. In order to represent God, they had to know His ways—as do we.

A Judgment of Serpents

In addition to the many ways we've already covered in which the Lord taught the Israelites to live by faith, we read of another experience in Numbers 21:4–9. The sons of Israel had left the Desert of Zin at Kadesh and travelled to Mount Hor, where Aaron died (Num. 20:22–29). Then, the Israelites "set out from Mount Hor by the way of the Red Sea, to go around the land of Edom; and the people became impatient because of the journey. The people spoke against God and Moses, 'Why have you brought us up out of Egypt to die in the wilderness? For there is no food and no water, and we loathe this miserable food'" (Num. 21:4–5). Such complaints among the Israelites were common on their journey. Obviously, they still had not learned God's ways. The Lord was testing the faith of His people, but they did not realize they were in the school of life.

So judgment came. "The LORD sent fiery serpents among the people and they bit the people, so that many people of Israel died" (v. 6). When the people saw the judgment of the Lord, they recognized their faults and made their confession to Moses. "So the people came to Moses and said, 'We have sinned, because we have spoken against the Lord and you; intercede with the Lord, that He may remove the serpents from us.' And Moses interceded for the people" (v. 7).

In answer to Moses' prayer, the Lord provided the solution: "Then the LORD said to Moses, 'Make a fiery serpent, and set it on a standard; and it shall come about, that everyone who is bitten, when he looks at it, he will live. And Moses made a bronze serpent and set it on the standard; and it came about, that if a serpent bit any man, when he looked to the bronze serpent, he lived'" (21:8–9).

The bronze serpent was a type of the judgment of our sins. The crucifixion of the Lord Jesus Christ was the fulfillment of the type. Notice that the healing came from obeying the Lord by looking at the bronze serpent, not from the bronze serpent itself. Jesus said, "As Moses lifted up the serpent in the wilderness, even so must the Son of Man be lifted up; so that whoever believes will in Him have eternal life" (John 3:14). Those who look to the Lord Jesus to save them from the judgment of sin will be saved. The Lord, Himself, used this wilderness experience of the Israelites as another way to recognize the work of the cross.

In 1 Corinthians 10:9, the apostle Paul also used this incident as another warning of improper Christian activity with the charge, "Nor let us try the Lord, as some of them did, and were destroyed by the serpents."

Moving Toward Milk and Honey

The sons of Israel had to wander in the wilderness for forty years before they could enter the land of milk and honey. During this time, the Lord would continue training them in the "school of life" and reinforce the lessons of trust. They had to learn to obey Him. Obedience demonstrates trust. All they had to do was look at the bronze serpent; just look. Likewise, all we have to do is focus on the Lord Jesus and what He did on the cross at Calvary; just look. When we understand that we never stop learning the need for faith, we have reached another milestone in our journey toward becoming a Milk and Honey Man.

CHAPTER 18

Baalam and Baal of Peor

Craving Evil Things

NUMBERS 25:1–9

AFTER MANY YEARS of wandering through the wilderness, the Israelites finally seemed to be moving in the direction of the place where they would cross the Jordan. There seemed to be "light at the end of the tunnel." Were they finally drawing near the end of their pilgrimage? Perhaps, but they still had to go through territory occupied by foreign nations to get there. They had to get past the Amorites and the people of Bashan and Moab.

The Amorites

When the sons of Israel reached the land inhabited by the Amorites, they sent messengers to Sihon, king of the Amorites, requesting that he allow them to pass through his territory. They told the king they would not venture into his fields or vineyard or drink the water from the wells. They promised to go by the king's highway until they had passed through the Amorites' border (Num. 21:21–22). The sons of Israel were trying to avoid a fight.

Unfortunately, Sihon would not permit them to pass through his land. "So Sihon gathered all his people and went out against Israel in the wilderness, and came to Jahaz and fought against Israel. Then Israel struck him with the edge of the sword, and took possession of his land from the Arnon [river] to the Jabbok [river], as far as the sons of Ammon; for the border of the sons of Ammon was Jazer" (Num. 21:23–24).

The sons of Israel took possession of the cities of the Amorites, including Heshbon, the city of Sihon, king of the Amorites, and its surrounding settlements (Num. 21:25–26). We don't know how long the Israelites were there, but it seems evident by this time that they were purposefully moving toward the Promised Land. There was even a prophecy about the taking of Moab (Num. 21:28–29).

The Lord was sharpening the Israelites' military skills in order to prepare them for the conquest of the Promised Land. The next battle would be with the people of Bashan.

Bashan

The sons of Israel turned and went along the road toward Bashan. There, they were met by Og[46], the king of Bashan, who marched out with his people to do battle against them at a place called Edrei (Num. 21:33). The Lord said to Moses, "Do not fear him, for I have given him into your hand, and all his people and his land; and you shall do to him as you did to Sihon, king of the Amorites, who lived at Heshbon" (v. 34). So the sons of Israel killed him and his sons and all his people and took hold of his land (v. 35).

These two victories built up the Israelites' confidence and prepared them to conquer the land ahead. Moses told the Israelites that the Lord had accomplished these victories and that they could depend on Him to give them similar victories when they had reached the Promised Land (Deut. 3:21). If they could only go past Moab peacefully …

Moab and Baalam

Having seen the total destruction of the two previous nations, the Moabites were understandably fearful that they would be the next to be conquered by the sons of Israel (Num. 22:3). So Balak, king of the Moabites, sent messengers to a man named Balaam, saying, "Behold, a people came out of Egypt; behold, they cover the surface of the land, and they are living opposite me. Now, therefore, please come, curse this people for me since they are too mighty for me; perhaps I may be able to defeat them and drive them out of the land. For I know that he whom you bless is blessed, and he whom you curse is cursed" (vv. 5–6).

Balak sent the elders with "fees for divination in their hand" (v. 7). However, God told Balaam not to heed the summons and go to Balak, because the Israelites were blessed. Thus, he refused to go. So Balak sent for him a second time with the promise he would be richly rewarded, and this time, after talking to the Lord again, Balaam went. On the way, the Lord sent an angel with a sword to stand in a narrow path between two vineyards with walls on both sides. When Balaam's donkey saw the angel, she pressed close to the wall, crushing Balaam's foot. Balaam even had a conversation with the donkey, until the Lord opened his eyes and allowed him to see the angel (Num. 22:21–34).

The Lord allowed Balaam to continue on his journey, but He told Balaam to speak only what He told him to say. So Balaam met Balak at the city of Moab, and there was taken to three different high places. Each time, Balaam blessed the Israelites instead of cursing them. He started off at "one of the high places of Baal" (Num. 22:41), an indication that spiritual war was going on and that Satan was going to try to attack the sons of Israel.

Balak was quite angry after these events, and he dismissed Balaam. Subsequently, Balaam took up a discourse, which included the following prophecy: "A star shall come forth from Jacob, a scepter shall rise from Israel, and shall crush through the forehead of Moab, and tear down all the sons of Sheth"[47] (Num. 24:17). After giving this prophecy, Baalam returned to his home, and Balak also went his way (Num. 24:25).

Baal of Peor

Balaam was motivated by money (2 Peter 2:15). He quickly realized he could not curse a nation already blessed by God, for with the Lord's blessing comes the Lord's divine protection. However, Balaam also knew if you stripped the people of their righteousness (that is, led them into sin), you could remove this divine protection. With that kind of advice, Balaam became an expensive and effective consultant (Num. 31:16).

While the Israelites were staying at a place called Shittim, "the people began to play the harlot with the daughters of Moab. For they invited the people to the sacrifices of their gods, and the people ate and bowed down to their gods. So Israel joined themselves to Baal of Peor [the local version of Baal], and the LORD was angry against Israel" (Num. 25:1–3). In Psalm 106:28 we read, "They joined themselves also to Baal-Peor, and ate sacrifices to the dead."

Thus, the Lord brought judgment on the Israelites. He instructed Moses to take all of the leaders of the people and execute them in broad daylight. In this way, His fierce anger would be turned away from Israel. So Moses said to the judges of Israel, "Each of you slay his men who have joined themselves to Baal of Peor" (Num. 25:4–5).

As the Israelites were weeping at the entrance to the Tent of Meeting over this latest judgment, an Israelite man named Zimri arrived with a Midianite woman named Cozbi, who was the daughter of the leader of Midian. There, before Moses and the entire assembly, Zimri takes Cozbi into a tent with him. When a priest named Phinehas (a grandson of Aaron) sees this, he picks up a spear, follows the couple into the tent, and drives the spear through both of them.

The Lord tells Moses, "Phinehas the son of Eleazar, the son of Aaron the priest, has turned away My wrath from the sons of Israel in that he was jealous with My jealousy among them, so that I did not destroy the sons of Israel in My jealousy" (Num. 25:11). Phinehas's action halts the plague against the sons of Israel, but not before 24,000 are killed (Num. 25:9). In 1 Corinthians 10:8, Paul recorded the number at 23,000, which could indicate that the leaders totaled 1,000.

God's command to the sons of Israel to not commit adultery and to have no other gods before Him was nothing new. Although the sons of Israel were getting close to their destination, it seems there were some Israelites (like Zimri) who were not ready for God's blessing of milk and honey. A Promised Land person will live by faith—a faith that is reflected in obedience. Again, as Paul wrote, "These things happened as examples for us, so that we would not crave evil things as they also craved" (1 Cor. 10:6).

Moving Toward Milk and Honey

When the sons of Israel were getting close to their destination, Satan tried to pull them down and rob them of their victory. The same applies to believers who are seeking victory in Jesus today. False gods like Baal were not allowed for the Israelites, and they are not allowed for believers. Adultery was not allowed for them, and it is not allowed for us. Remember this as you approach victory, and you will have reached another milestone.

CHAPTER 19

Crossing the Jordan River
Identification with Christ
JOSHUA 3:10–17

WHERE WERE THE Israelites headed? When Moses, after his personal wilderness experience, met God in the burning bush, the Lord said to him regarding the sons of Israel, "I have come down [from heaven] to deliver them from the power of the Egyptians, and to bring them up from that land to a good and spacious land, to a land flowing with milk and honey, to the place of the Canaanite,[48] and the Hittite, and the Amorite, and the Perrizite, the Hivite, and the Jebusite" (Ex. 3:8). God's destiny for the Israelites from the first time He expressed His intentions to Moses was to deliver them from bondage in Egypt.

When they were about to cross the Red Sea, Moses again told them of their destination: "It shall be when the Lord brings you into the land of the Canaanite, the Hittite, the Amorite, the Hivite, and the Jebusite which He swore to your fathers to give you, a land flowing with milk and honey" (Ex. 13:5). The land flowing with milk and honey was the destination of the sons of Israel!

The Israelites' forty years of wandering the desert were finished. All of those who had been unwilling to go into the Promised Land at Kadesh-Barnea had died. Joshua had been appointed to replace Moses, and he was in the process of learning how to become leader of the people. God said to Joshua, "Cross this Jordan [River], you and all this people, to the land which I am giving to them, to the sons of Israel" (Josh. 1:2). This was a command from God. It included the promise that He was giving them the land. In this case, He was referring to occupancy of the land.

As the sons of Israel stood at the banks of the Jordan, their feet wet from the flooding of the river and the ark of the covenant nearby, they faced a crisis of faith. Would they believe this time? Would they trust the Lord to bring them into the Promised Land—a land that seemed to be inhabited by giants? They had been delivered out of bondage in Egypt. Could they be delivered into a new life in the Promised Land?

Map of the Pilgrimage

The following diagram is the fourth chronological "map" that compares the physical journey of the sons of Israel to those taking the pilgrimage of the Christian life in the twenty-first century. As you will recall, the sons of Israel received and committed to the Mosaic Covenant and the Mosaic Law at Mt. Sinai. Subsequently several negative events occurred, events which seemed to have a stronger punishment aspect.

The first of these events came after only one month had gone by—the Israelites became concerned that Moses would not return down from the mount and convinced Aaron to create a golden calf that they could worship. By doing so, the sons of Israel broke the first two of the Ten Commandments that the Lord had given to them.

After leaving Mt. Sinai, they arrived at Kadesh-Barnea, the place from which they would enter into the Promised Land. (As the map indicates, about eighteen months had now passed since the time they had crossed the Red Sea.) Twelve spies were sent out to evaluate the land and its people. The spies brought back a good report on the land—it was indeed a land flowing with "milk and honey"—and two of the spies, Joshua and Caleb, encouraged the people to go forward into the land with the help of the Lord. However, the other ten spies felt that they could not take the land. They told the people, "All the people whom we saw … are men of great size … and we became like grasshoppers in our own sight" (Num. 13:32–33). In the end, the majority ruled. So God judged the people for their lack of faith and told them that they would wander in the wilderness for forty years. This was the place of the second negative event.

Later, in the third such event, the sons of Israel again reached a place in which there was no water to drink. God instructed Moses to speak to the rock, but he grew angry with the people and disobeyed God. Instead of speaking to the rock, he struck the rock twice, and this action sent a wrong message to the generations to come. Because of his disobedience,

CHRONOLOGICAL MAP
CROSSING THE THIRD THRESHOLD

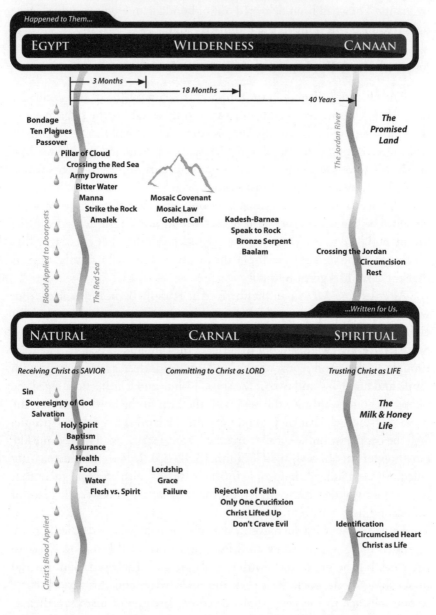

Happened to Them...

EGYPT   **WILDERNESS**   **CANAAN**

← 3 Months →
← 18 Months →
← 40 Years →

The Jordan River

Bondage
Ten Plagues
Passover
  Pillar of Cloud
  Crossing the Red Sea
  Army Drowns
  Bitter Water
  Manna
  Strike the Rock
  Amalek

Mosaic Covenant
Mosaic Law
Golden Calf

Kadesh-Barnea
Speak to Rock
Bronze Serpent
Baalam

**The
Promised
Land**

Crossing the Jordan
Circumcision
Rest

Blood Applied to Doorposts

The Red Sea

...Written for Us.

NATURAL   **CARNAL**   **SPIRITUAL**

Receiving Christ as SAVIOR   *Committing to Christ as LORD*   *Trusting Christ as LIFE*

Sin
Sovereignty of God
Salvation
  Holy Spirit
  Baptism
  Assurance
  Health
  Food
  Water
  Flesh vs. Spirit

Lordship
Grace
Failure

Rejection of Faith
Only One Crucifixion
Christ Lifted Up
Don't Crave Evil

**The
Milk & Honey
Life**

Identification
Circumcised Heart
Christ as Life

Christ's Blood Applied

130

God prohibited Moses from entering the Promised Land. There would be no milk and honey for Moses.

Fourth, the Israelites grew impatient with their circumstances and complained against Moses, and God judged them by sending fiery serpents. The only cure for those who had received the serpents' deadly bites was to look upon a standard of a bronze serpent that God had instructed Moses to create. In this way, the people were delivered from death. The bronze serpent would prove to be a type of the Lord Jesus hanging on the cross.

Finally, when the sons of Israel attempted to pass Moab, they were enticed into relations with the Moabite and Midianite women and their god, Baal of Peor. It was only after 24,000 people had died that the deadly plague from the Lord was brought to an end.

Defensive or Offensive?

It often seems easier to trust God for deliverance when the enemy is breathing down our necks and we have no obvious option other than to trust Him. In these situations, we are on the defensive. It is more difficult to trust Him when we are on the offensive—when we are going into enemy territory. The experience of this generation of the sons of Israel teaches us a lesson of faith. At this point, as they stood by the flooded river, they intended to conquer the land by faith. There is a difference in how we approach obedience by faith.

The previous generation had had their backs against the wall when they left Egypt. Even though God had set them apart in Egypt for 400 years, had performed ten miracles that proved He was more powerful than the Egyptian false gods, and even though they knew they were the Lord's Chosen People, they had still left Egypt on the defense. The Egyptian army had chased them after they left and were hot on their tail. The sons of Israel had a destiny, but they had no idea what the route would be or how long it would take to get there. When the water parted, they just had to follow Moses and trust in the Lord. There was no other possibility.

However, at the Jordan River, the sons of Israel were now on the offense. They were going into the Promised Land and were planning to attack the various nations on their own territory. The Israelites did not know how the enemy operated, what the military conditions would be, or what they would face. This time, they would need to trust the Lord for victory.

When I began to grow as a Christian, I was taught by the Lord about the need to trust Him. I learned that He "ran the bank." He was in charge of money and provision of food, shelter, clothes, transportation, and so forth. I discovered He would control what my wife and I did by the provision of or withholding of funds. God owns everything and determines how much or what we get to use.

On two occasions, my wife and I received unsolicited, anonymous gifts of cash in our mailbox in specific amounts for our situation at the time. Both of these cash gifts were related to the advancement of God's kingdom. This was offensive faith in that it enabled us to move forward. He provided for our efforts in evangelism. Unlike defensive faith—which would include the times when faith is needed to face situations such as when you are struggling to pay bills, or your health is in trouble, or your kids are in jail, or whenever you don't have a solution to the problem. An offensive faith expands the kingdom of God. It includes neighborhood witnessing, foreign missions, one-on-one evangelism, and the like.

God's Rest

The Promised Land was called "God's rest." In Genesis 2:1, we read that after six days of creation, God rested from His works. The place of "rest" is a place (or a circumstance) a believer can "enter" (Heb. 3:19) that allows, enables, and even demands the believer to rest from his works (or self-effort). For the sons of Israel, this referred to the territory where they would accomplish God's will without "working." They would live by faith, not works. They would not do the work; the Lord would. They would be obedient, but the Lord would be the One Who would make things happen.

We should not be surprised by this. The gospel of John tells us that one time when the crowd was following Jesus, they asked Him, "What shall we do, so that we may work the works of God?"

Jesus answered, "This is the work of God, that you believe in Him whom He has sent" (John 6:28–29). I don't know about you, but I always thought that this passage was about salvation. However, while the inclusion of initial salvation is certainly there, it also includes living that way. As Paul stated in Romans 1:17, "The righteous man shall live by faith." We rest by trusting, believing in, and depending on the Lord Jesus.

Absolute Surrender

Let's say a Christian says he has made a total commitment. He has made a Lordship commitment—a Romans 12:1 commitment. "If it is in the Scripture, I will do it," he says. Great! But, who is doing the doing? He has given his money, his wallet, and his bank account to God. Good! But has he given God his job? If he is married, has he given his wife and his children to the Lord? If he is seeking to marry, has he given the Lord the decision of whether or not he will get married—and, if so, whom he will marry? It's risky! A Christian has to trust God completely.

In 1 Kings 20:1–4, we read the story of how Ahab, king of Israel (the northern ten tribes), made an act of absolute surrender. Unfortunately, this act of surrender was not to God.

> Now Ben-hadad king of Aram gathered all his army, and there were thirty-two kings with him, and horses and chariots. And he went up and besieged Samaria and fought against it. Then he sent messengers to the city to Ahab king of Israel and said to him, "Thus says Ben-hadad, 'Your silver and gold are mine; your most beautiful wives and children are also mine.' The king of Israel replied, 'It is according to your word, my lord, O King; I am yours, and all that I have.'"

King Ahab made a total surrender to a foreign king—a human being. We should sell out that way to the King of Creation, but not to another human, regardless of whether that person is an enemy or friend.

When the Israelites were at Mt. Sinai, they made a total commitment to God. They promised they would do all God had said. But, as we have seen, they blew it on several occasions and failed to keep their promise. They did not trust in the Lord. They did not exercise faith.

It was one thing for the sons of Israel to exercise faith that the path through the Red Sea would stay open when Pharaoh's army was on their heels. They had no other choice—they had to have faith in God. However, it was quite another matter for them to exercise faith when they are on the other side of the equation; that is, when they were the ones who were supposed to go into the battle. In such situations, the natural response is to put one's faith in military superiority, and that is what they did when they were at Kadesh-Barnea.

Furthermore, the Israelites' commitment at Mt. Sinai was one of "we will do what God says to do." But now they had come to the Promised Land—the place of "God's rest"—where God had to do the doing. It has always been this way. Jesus is not just the boss who tells us what to do, but also the Lord Who does it through us. He sets the targets, the strategy, and the timing. We are here to do His will, not our will. We are to accomplish

His goals, not our goals, and to do it His way, not our way. Believers are to be a kingdom of priests for Him. We are to do everything for His glory, not our own personal glory. And we are to trust Him to do the doing.

Once we as believers arrive in the land of milk and honey, we can represent Christ in the world. We are His "bondservants." A bondservant is one who has been set free from being a slave but, due to his love and respect for his master, voluntarily chooses to stay and serve his master. The Master wants to live His life through us. We submit to Him not because we are required to do so, but because we want to do so. We voluntarily serve.

Identification

Before the sons of Israel made preparations to enter the Promised Land, Joshua, the new leader of God's people, sent two spies to look over the land (Josh. 2:1). They stayed at the house of Rahab, the prostitute, and talked with her. Rahab said to them,

> I know that the LORD has given you the land, and that the terror of you has fallen on us, and that all the inhabitants of the land have melted away before you. For we have heard how the LORD dried up the water of the Red Sea before you when you came out of Egypt, and what you did to the two kings of the Amorites who were beyond the Jordan, to Sihon and Og, whom you utterly destroyed. When we heard it, our hearts melted and no courage remained in any man because of you; for the LORD your God, He is God in heaven above and on earth beneath.
>
> —Josh. 2:9–11

The Canaanites knew that the sons of Israel were marching toward them. They knew about God's power and that the Lord was taking care of the Israelites. In other words, they had identified the sons of Israel with their God. His power was the source of their success. His attributes represented their attributes. His commandments shaped their values. His goals were their goals. The Israelites were immersed in their identification with Him—and, for this reason, the residents of Jericho had great fear of them. After forty years of wandering in the desert, God's chosen people had acquired an identity as God's chosen people. It was general knowledge in the world.

What is your identity? Or, to put it a different way, who are you? Imagine you are at some kind of meeting where nobody in the room knows anybody else. You are all strangers to one another. The leader or moderator says, "We are going to go around the room and have each person stand up, give us your name, and tell us a little about yourself—tell us who you are." What would you say?

Think about the factors that have influenced and formed your personal identity at each of the various stages of your life. As a child, your primary influencers were probably your parents. As an adolescent, it was possibly your peers. As an adult, you have certainly received some influence from your profession. In fact, a job or career is frequently the item by which most people will identify themselves: "I am an engineer." "I am a nurse." "I am a lawyer."

There are other factors that will affect your identity. For example, being the child of someone famous or having some other personal relationship can affect your identity: "I am the child of President Kennedy." "I am a good friend of the mayor." Being proficient in a sport can affect your identity: "I am a Heisman trophy winner." "I am on the school's bowling team." On the flip side, being convicted of a felony or having some other known vice can affect your identity in a negative way: "I am a pickpocket." "I am the town drunk." "I am a registered sex offender."

However, as a Christian you have a different identity. As Paul states in 2 Corinthians 5:17, "Therefore if anyone is in Christ, he is a new creature; the old things passed away; behold, new things have come." You are a new creation; you are not who you were. You used to be a child in the Smith, Jones, Johnson, or Troth family. Now, if you are a Christian, you are identified with a new family: "I am a child of God." As Jesus states in the high priestly prayer in John 17:21–23, you are now one with Him. You identify with Him: "I am a Christian."

In Hebrews 11:13, we read that Abraham, Moses, and many other Old Testament heroes of the faith "confessed that they were strangers and exiles on the earth." They lived by faith as citizens of heaven. In 1 Peter 2:11, we find that we are also "aliens and strangers" to this world. We are sojourners who are just passing through—we are not identified with this world. We are children of God (1 John 3:4–10), and our conduct reflects who we are.

Christians now identify with Jesus Christ. We were crucified with Jesus Christ (Rom. 6:6; Gal. 2:20). We have been baptized into His death (Rom. 6:3). We were buried with Jesus Christ (Rom. 6:4). We were resurrected with Him (Rom. 6:4–5; Eph. 2:6). We have been raised up with Him and seated in heavenly places with Him (Eph. 2:6).

These things that happened to Him also happened to you, so that you can now say, "I am a Christian. It is my identity."

Death of Self

Jesus' words in John 12:24 teach us the significance of death: "Truly, truly, I say to you, unless a grain of wheat falls into the earth and dies, it remains alone; but if it dies, it bears much fruit." An operational expression of this statement follows in the next verse: "He who loves his life loses it, and he who hates his life in this world will keep it to life eternal" (v. 25).

Pastor Jack Taylor relates the following illustration of the necessity of death:

> In a tree there is a type of vascular tissue called the xylem. This type of cell is used to bring minerals and water, the life-giving substance of a tree, to the various parts of the tree from the ground. The unique thing about these cells is that they are of no use to the tree until they are dead. In a living cell there is cytoplasm and the nucleus which is the cell nature. As long as this nature lives it blocks the flow of life-giving substances that are so desperately needed by the tree.[49]

What happened at the cross? Jesus was crucified! And so were we! Romans 6:6 reveals that "our old self [old man] was crucified with Him." We are to act on that fact. In Romans 6:11, we are instructed to "consider [ourselves] to be dead to sin." The KJV uses the word "reckon" in place of consider: "reckon ye also yourselves to be dead indeed unto sin." We are to set a course for our lives based on this fact that we have died. We need to agree with God and live according to that reality.

Death is the only means we have of being delivered from self. We cannot kill ourselves and God does not want us to do so. He does, however, want us to believe what His Word says about our death. It happened. We were crucified with Christ.

If we are going to represent the Lord—if we are going to be a kingdom of priests and glorify God—we have to die. Our assignment is to represent Jesus, to bring Him glory, and Jesus is the best person to represent Jesus. Therefore, we must be dead to self.

If you are a believer, this has already happened to you. Now you just need to consider it so. Operate your life on the basis that you are dead so that Christ's life can flow through you.

Christ as Life

In fact, there are two people in your body—your "earthsuit"—you and Jesus, or, expressed another way, your "self" and the Holy Spirit. Which one is going to live the life? Who is going to be in charge? Who will be the decision maker? And who is the most skilled at interpersonal relations?

You might ask a well-studied student of the Bible, "Why are we here?" Perhaps he or she will correctly say, "To glorify God!" How do we do this? In Colossians 1:26–27, the apostle Paul wrote of "the mystery hidden from the past ages and generations, but has now been manifested to His saints … which is Christ in you, the hope of glory." The only hope we have of bringing glory to Jesus is by the fact of His being in us.

Amazing as it may seem, "Christ is even more than our Savior and Lord; He is also our very Life."[50] In Colossians 3:3–4, Paul wrote, "You have died and your life is hidden with Christ in God. When Christ, who is our life, is revealed, then you also will be revealed with Him in glory." Likewise, when Jesus spoke to Martha about her brother, Lazarus, He said, "I am the resurrection and the life; he who believes in Me will live even if he dies, and everyone who lives and believes in Me will never die" (John 11:25–26). Jesus is the very life of those who believe, and that is what He gives us—life eternal.

Paul describes this process in Galatians 2:20: "I [the one long-known as the driver of this earthsuit] have been crucified [I am now dead and can't drive very well—but then, I never could] with Christ; and it is no longer I who live, but Christ lives in me, and the life which I now live in the flesh [this earthsuit] I live by faith [I trust Jesus as driver] in the Son of God who loved me and gave Himself up for Me." Some folks sing, "He came from heaven to earth, to show the way …" but might I suggest that Jesus came from heaven to earth to be the way. Scripture says that He is "the way, and the truth, and the life" (John 14:6). He is not limited to showing us how to live. He is the way! He wants to live through us.

Dr. Charles Solomon wrote, "God does not want us to work for Him, to witness for Him, to live for Him. He wants us to get self out of the way so He can work through us."[51] Dr. Solomon also notes, "Don't you ever try to live the Christian life! You have invited the Lord Jesus Christ into your life. Let Him live His life in you. That's why He entered your life."[52]

The Dividing Line

The Israelites finally arrived at the long-awaited Promised Land and were about to cross the Jordan River. At this point Joshua spoke to them and said, "When ... the feet of the priests who carry the ark of the LORD, the Lord of all the earth, rest in the waters of the Jordan, the waters of the Jordan will be cut off, and the waters which are flowing down from above will stand in one heap" (Josh. 3:13).

This came to pass just as Joshua had said. When the priests carrying the ark of the covenant stepped into the Jordan, the waters "stood and rose up in one heap" (Josh. 3:16). So the people crossed on land opposite the city of Jericho. The priests carrying the ark stood in the middle of the Jordan until all the people had finished crossing the river.

Crossing the Jordan River into the Promised Land was a major step in the history of the sons of Israel. At this pivotal moment, they changed status from pilgrims to settlers. They also changed from people exercising a defensive faith (faith to live) to ones who were exercising an offensive faith (faith to enhance God's kingdom). The Jordan River was a definite dividing line for the Israelites.

For twenty-first century Christians, crossing the dividing line occurs when a person changes from a carnal man to a spiritual man. However, the point of time when this occurs is not as clearly defined as when the sons of Israel completed their forty years of wandering in the wilderness, crossed the Jordan River, and went into the land of milk and honey. Some people describe the change as "progressive sanctification." They use that phrase because believers are continually growing toward spiritual maturity.

The distinction for believers between the categories of carnal and spiritual is not as precisely defined as it was experienced by the Israelites. For example, Hebrews 5:12 says some believers are only able to drink milk, while others are ready for solid food. But when does the transition occur? And even if a believer is ready for solid food, does that mean he has reached victory?

Furthermore, we know that some believers still need to be taught "the elementary doctrine of Christ" (Heb. 6:1 ESV) while others are able to teach. However, there is no biblical definition for how to identify a set of qualifications that define a person as moving from carnal to spiritual. There is no dividing line spelled out.

We have been set apart by God. We have been sanctified. But, at the same time, we are still being sanctified and will continue to be so until our ultimate sanctification (which, also, is referred to as glorification). And even though we are encouraged to do things that will help move us along the process toward maturity, ultimately, Christ is our Sanctifier, not self-effort.

Progressive Sanctification

The following diagram illustrates the concept of progressive sanctification. Notice in the diagram that there is a black circle below the line titled "justified." This represents a person who is still in his inherited sin. This person is unsaved. He is still in bondage to sin. He is a natural man.

At the top of the diagram, the white circle represents a Christian who is glorified. This takes place when he dies physically.

In the middle is a jagged line that represents growing toward maturity. Some would describe this as progressive sanctification. The person following this course will eventually end up at the perfect, glorified state, but there will be many setbacks along the way. Christians still sin, and sometimes in a major way.

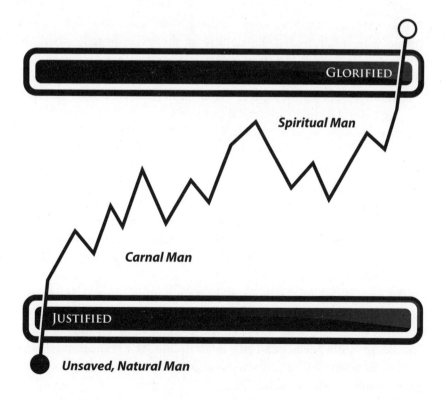

GLORIFIED

Spiritual Man

Carnal Man

JUSTIFIED

Unsaved, Natural Man

Observing the diagram, where would you put the line to distinguish between a carnal man and a spiritual man? That question presents the difficulty of trying to establish a dividing line.

Suppose the question is defining when a person knows or experiences identification with Christ. How much does a person have to know or experience in order to move from being carnal to being spiritual? How well must that individual understand the relationship? We know that each of us must live by faith, but how deep must that faith be for us to be considered spiritual? The dividing line is not as precise as crossing a river.

Another difficulty for us is the fact that the typology used in *The Milk and Honey Man* begins with a type of a nation in the Old Testament and is fulfilled by individuals in the New Testament. The point here is that the rate or pattern of spiritual growth varies from one Christian to the next.

The Flesh and the Spirit

In Chapter 11, "The Battle of the Flesh and the Spirit," we presented two diagrams showing, first, a person being flesh-controlled, and, second, a person who is Spirit-filled. Previously, we showed a diagram where the spirit of man (represented by the inner circle) goes from black to white. This change refers to that person's position—he is now a child of God—but in the diagram on the previous page, the black-filled circle below the line is depicting a non-Christian (again, his position).

Just as the sons of Israel repeatedly battled the Amalekites throughout their history, Christians continually struggle against the flesh. The diagrams in Chapter 11 are reproduced below on the next page. The color (black or white) of the inner circle here is intended to communicate the condition of an individual at any given point during his daily walk with Christ. He will either be controlled by the flesh (the black circle on the left) or filled with the Spirit (the white circle on the right). This explanation might help some readers appreciate Ephesians 5:18: "Do not get drunk with wine ... but be filled with the Spirit."

The jagged line in the progressive sanctification diagram indicates a length of time in the process of sanctification, but the possibility of instant spirituality does exist. This occurs on those occasions when you are Spirit-filled. Being Spirit-filled takes place in an instant, at a point in time. This would occur when Christ Who is in you is living His life through you—when you are trusting Christ-as-Life.[53]

Some see progressive sanctification as the path to victory. However, that is based on self-effort and is therefore no victory at all. Some have experienced benefits from focusing on what the blood of Christ has done for us. Scripture speaks of many benefits from His blood, and we certainly need to learn those truths and be mindful of them.

Another view is centered on our resurrection. Jesus was resurrected from the dead and is alive. We were crucified with Christ, dead with Christ, buried with Christ, and raised with Christ (Rom. 6:3–6). Furthermore, we have been seated in the heavenly places with Christ (Eph. 2:6). These are two important aspects of what Jesus has done for us. The key, however, is that we need to exercise faith in the Lord. That is what got the generation of Israelites that occupied the Promised Land across the Jordan River.

Some Christians, unknowingly, put their faith in their own ability (or their "self"). They are a "selfer"—one who lives by the power of the flesh. They need to become a "lifer"—one who lives by Jesus' life within them. The flesh-controlled life and Spirit-filled life diagrams are applicable here. Jesus Christ is not only the Savior and the Lord, but He is also the Life. When we understand these truths and commit ourselves to them, it leads to a victorious life.

If the Lord has convinced you that you are a selfer (a person who makes the final decision for his or her life or one who executes the control of his or her life), and if you believe that Jesus is supposed shine through, then here is a prayer you might want to pray:

> Lord Jesus, I confess I have been living by the power of my flesh, rather than by the power of Your life. Break me of self-capability. Reveal to me

my "self" and Your "life." Cause me and enable me to live by the power of Your Spirit. I ask these things in Your name.

If you prayed that prayer, I encourage you to sign on the line below and to tell someone about it.

_____   _____

Your Name   Date

Moving Toward Milk and Honey

Jesus is the Savior of the world ("We have seen and testify that the Father has sent the Son to be the Savior of the world," 1 John 4:14), but He will not be your Savior until you, personally, apply the blood He shed on the cross on your behalf. You must place your trust in Him for Him to become your Savior.

Jesus is also the Lord of the world ("The God who made the world and everything in it is the Lord of heaven and earth," Acts 17:24 NIV), but He will not be your Lord until you, personally, commit to His sovereign rule in your life. You must commit to obedience to His commands for Him to become your Lord.

Finally, Jesus is the Life of the world ("I am the way, and the truth, and the life," John 14:6), but He will not be your life until you, personally, recognize that truth. You must surrender to His rule through your body for Him to become your life.

Let me know if you cross these thresholds, and I will celebrate with you as you taste the milk and honey.

O taste and see that the Lord is good; How blessed is the man that takes refuge in Him!

—Ps. 34:8

CHAPTER 20

Circumcision in the Promised Land

Circumcision of the Heart

GENESIS 17:9–27; JOSHUA 5:2–9

THE ISRAELITES HAD crossed the Jordan River and were now in the Promised Land. However, before they could conquer the land, there was another task they had to do first. As a sign of their identification with the Lord—a sign of the unique bond they had with their Deliverer—the men of the whole nation of Israel were required to be circumcised. This circumcision took place right after the sons of Israel had crossed the Jordan River, and it indicated a new beginning for them—a fresh start as the chosen people of God. The Israelites would live with the recognition that the Lord was in the driver's seat.

One might consider the subject of circumcision a "postscript" for the Egypt-to-Canaan pilgrimage, since the Israelites were in the Promised Land. This took place after "the forty year wanderers" went through the process of circumcisions. However, the act of circumcision might well be considered a "prologue" because the practice began with the covenant between God and Abraham in Genesis 17—long before the Egypt-to-Canaan pilgrimage began.

The book of Joshua records the Lord's instruction to Joshua to circumcise the sons of Israel a "second time" (Josh. 5:2). Because one cannot remove the foreskins a second time, the instruction to the nation was, in effect, to circumcise the men of the nation again. None of the Israelite males who had been born en route to the Promised Land had been circumcised during the trek through the wilderness. "This is the reason why Joshua circumcised them: all the males of the people who came out of Egypt, all the men of war, had died in the wilderness on the way after they had come out of Egypt. ... all the people who were born on the way in the wilderness after they had come out of Egypt had not been circumcised" (Josh 5:4–5 ESV). Of course, because Joshua and Caleb were among the generation that had left Egypt, they were already circumcised.

A Desire for Offspring

At the time of creation, the Lord God had a goal: He wanted offspring. The creation of man ended with the injunction, "Let Us make man [mankind] in Our image, according to Our likeness" (Gen. 1:26). After doing so, He blessed them and said, "Be fruitful and multiply, and fill the earth" (v. 28).

When God called Abram, He told him to leave his country and said that He would make Abram into a great nation (Gen. 12:2). Abram and Sarai had not had any children, so Abram suggested to the Lord that his servant Eliezer fill the role of his heir. But the Lord said, "This man will not be your heir; but one who will come forth from your own body, he shall be your heir" (Gen. 15:4).

Later, Abram's wife, Sarai, took matters into her own hands and told Abram to have relations with her maid, Hagar, so Sarai might obtain children through her (Gen. 16:2). Abram had relations with Hagar, and Ishmael was born. However, he was a child of the flesh (Gal. 4:23), and the Lord told Hagar he would be "a wild donkey of a man, his hand against everyone and everyone's hand against him, and he shall dwell over against all his kinsmen" (Gen. 16:12 ESV). After this, the Lord established the covenant with Abram and changed his name to Abraham.

Notice the sequence:

1. God gave the exhortation to have offspring (a spiritual calling).
2. Abram failed to produce offspring (a spiritual test).
3. Abram suggested that Eliezer be his heir (a fleshly idea).
4. God promised Abram children from his own body (a spiritual plan).
5. Sarai suggested an alternative plan to produce an heir (a fleshly idea).
6. Abraham fathered Ishmael by Hagar (a fleshly act).
7. The Lord said Ishmael would persecute Isaac (an indication of his flesh).
8. God changed Abram's name and established the covenant of circumcision (a spiritual plan).

The practice of circumcision did not begin until the establishment of a family of faith. That occasion occurred with the announcement that Abram and Sarai were to have a child from Sarai's body, and when God changed Abram's name (meaning "exalted father") to Abraham (meaning "father of a multitude"). Abraham was to be "exceedingly fruitful" (Gen. 17:6), and circumcision was to be the sign of this covenant with God (Gen. 17:11). God was to make Abraham and his descendants fruitful—and indeed He did. When seventy-five Israelites moved into Goshen in the land of Egypt, they multiplied into 600,000 men of military age (which is easily a community of two to three million). That increase took only 400 years!

Removing the Flesh

Circumcision is the removal of the foreskin of the male sexual organ. Because God could have made males without the foreskin, it seems that He required this practice of the sons of Israel to teach the people an important truth. Furthermore, although there is some medical benefit to the practice,[54] it has been said that this was not the primary reason for circumcision.

During circumcision, the flesh around the male sexual organ is removed. Removal of the flesh from this organ of multiplication seems to symbolize the spiritual benefit of eradicating the flesh in our lives, as we discussed in Chapter 11 when we examined the battle between the flesh and the Spirit (the sons of Israel and the Amalekites). God does not want us to depend on our flesh (human effort) for multiplication, as Abram and Sarai did. Even the sexual relationship between a husband and wife can and should be a spiritual matter.

Later, in the book of Malachi, we again hear of the Lord's desire for offspring. In Malachi 2:14–15 (ESV), the Lord tells the prophet He does not regard the offering of Judah. Malachi explains,

> You say, "Why does he not?" Because the Lord was witness between you and the wife of your youth, to whom you have been faithless, though she is your companion and your wife by covenant. Did he not make them one, with a portion of the Spirit in their union? And what was the one God seeking? Godly offspring. So guard yourselves in your spirit, and let none of you be faithless to the wife of your youth.

God not only wants offspring, but He also wants godly offspring. And we also see He wants husbands to be faithful to their wives.

Prior to the Israelites' entry into the Promised Land, Moses reviewed the events of the wilderness pilgrimage. He said to the people:

> Now, Israel, what does the LORD your God require from you, but to fear the LORD your God, to walk in all His ways and love Him, and to serve the LORD your God with all your heart and with all your soul, and to keep the LORD's commandments and His statutes which I am commanding you today for your good?
>
> Behold, to the LORD your God belong heaven and the highest heavens, the earth and all that is in it. Yet on your fathers did the LORD set His affection to love them, and He chose their descendants after them, even you above all peoples, as it is this day. So circumcise your heart, and stiffen your neck no longer. For the LORD your God is the God of gods and the Lord of lords, the great, the mighty, and the awesome God who does not show partiality nor take a bribe. He executes justice for the orphan and the widow, and shows His love for the alien by giving him food and clothing. So show your love for the alien, for you were aliens in the land of Egypt.
>
> You shall fear the LORD your God; you shall serve Him and cling to Him, and you shall swear by His name. He is your praise and He is your God, who has done these great and awesome things for you which your eyes have seen. Your fathers went down to Egypt seventy persons in all, and now the Lord your God has made you as numerous as the stars of heaven.
>
> —Deut. 10:12–22

Notice that Moses tells the people that they should be circumcised in their hearts. This represents a spiritual condition—a removal of the flesh of the soul. He also tells them, "The Lord your God will circumcise your heart and the heart of your descendants, to love the LORD your God with all your heart and with all your soul, so that you may live" (Deut. 30:6).

The Lord is the One Who circumcises our hearts. He removes the flesh from us. The evidence of our obedience that we display as Christians who love our God reflects the Lord to other people. The character of our lives is supposed to make others see we belong to Jesus.

Those who trust Christ for salvation are "in Christ," and those who are in Christ were "circumcised with a circumcision made without hands, in the removal of the body of the flesh by the circumcision of Christ" (Col. 2:11). Circumcision has been credited to us as righteousness because we belong to Him. The Lord Jesus Christ is the righteousness of believers.

Moving Toward Milk and Honey

Before the sons of Israel could occupy the land, they needed to be circumcised. This practice was both a "sign" of their relationship with the true and living God and to remind them of the Lord's desire for godly offspring. In the same way, before you can occupy the land of milk and honey, you need to put off the flesh and have a circumcised heart. Only in this way can you become a soldier for the expansion of God's kingdom—the kingdom of milk and honey. Once you have, you have passed another milestone!

CHAPTER 21

Living in the Land of Milk and Honey

Rest for the Milk and Honey Man

1 PETER 1:1; HEBREWS 4

AT LONG LAST, the Israelites were in the Promised Land. They had reached the land of milk and honey—the land of God's rest. They would now rest in God's provision and God's direction.

The Covenant and the Land

More than 500 years prior to crossing the Jordan, the Lord had executed the Abrahamic covenant with Abram (his name at that time). Part of this promise included the gift of land. It was a unilateral promise, one-sided; only God had to perform. The Mosaic covenant between God and the Israelites, a bilateral, two-sided covenant, required obedience by the Israelites. The Israelites were to be God's own possession, a holy people, and a kingdom of priests. This generation could own the land:

- While going there (crossing the Red Sea in 1446 BC);
- When they arrived there (crossing the Jordan River in 1406 BC);
- When they were expelled and taken captive (to Syria in 722 BC and to Babylon in 605–586 BC);
- When they were allowed to go back (under Cyrus and Ezra in 539 BC and under Nehemiah in 444 BC);
- During the Diaspora (a "scattering" of the Jewish population beginning in AD 70); and

- When the nation of Israel was resettled and re-established (in AD 1948).

The Israelites must now complete the present-day reoccupation, for God's name is at stake!

Happened to Them

The Israelites were known as a people who belonged to the Lord. It was not a coincidence that the two spies, whom Joshua sent out, met and stayed at the home of Rahab the harlot (Josh. 2:1–21). Nor was it a coincidence that she was willing to hide them from the king of Jericho. She even encouraged them to conquer the territory when she said, "I know that the LORD has given you the land" (v. 9). She had heard how the Lord "dried up the water of the Red Sea" (v. 10) when they came out of Egypt. They already had a reputation of belonging to the Lord.

Furthermore, their trust and obedience reflected well on the Lord and revealed His power and authority to other peoples. Even as they made their pilgrimage from Egypt, fear fell on the people of the land. Rahab told the two spies, "When we heard of it, our hearts melted and everyone's courage failed because of you, for the LORD your God is God in heaven above and on the earth below" (v. 11 NIV). The spies heard through Rahab that this portion of the Mosaic covenant was being fulfilled.

Holy People

The Israelites were instructed by God to conquer the land. They were supposed to drive the Canaanites, the Hittites, the Amorites, the Perizzites, the Hivites, and the Jebusites out of the land. However, some foreigners (Gentiles) remained in the land. So the Israelites were instructed to not intermarry with these foreigners because "they will turn your sons away from following Me to serve other gods" (Deut. 7:4), and that would contaminate holiness. Of course, the Israelites had the Law, which demanded obedience to the moral laws. They were the representatives of a holy God!

A Kingdom of Priests

A "nation" was commonly referred to as a kingdom. In this case, the nation of the sons of Israel were to serve as a kingdom of priests. This included teaching the Law, interpreting it, applying it, serving the Lord, and leading in worship and intercession. Although the Israelite priests did that for the Israelites, there seems to be a sense that the sons of Israel had a role in influencing the foreigners among them.

Written for Us

The apostle Peter, writing to a wide range of first century Jewish believers in Christ, referred to them as "a chosen race, a royal priesthood, a holy nation, a people for God's own possession" (1 Peter 2:9).[55] From this, we see that the assignment of the Mosaic covenant applies to us. Likewise, we are told that Christ Jesus "gave Himself for us to redeem us from every lawless deed, and to purify for Himself a people for His own possession, zealous for good deeds" (Titus 2:14).

Several New Testament verses combine the aspect of being holy with being one of God's people. For instance, 1 Peter 2:10 states, "Once you were not a people, but now you are the people of God; you had not received mercy, but now you have received mercy." In other words, Peter was saying that now that we have been saved, we are Christians.

Holy People

There are numerous calls for Christians to be holy. In 1 Peter 2:11–12, the apostle said, "Beloved, I urge you as aliens and strangers to abstain from fleshly lusts which wage war against the soul. Keep your behavior excellent among the Gentiles, so that in the thing in which they slander you as evildoers, they may because of your good deeds, as they observe them, glorify God in the day of visitation." Christians are sometimes described as "saints," which means "holy ones." They are also described as "righteous."

A Kingdom of Priests

Being a "kingdom of priests" refers to Christians reaching out to non-Christians to bring them to God. In that responsibility, we should act upon the divine instruction given to us by Christ in Matthew 28:18–20: "All authority has been given to Me in heaven and on earth. Go therefore and make disciples of all the nations, baptizing them in the name of the Father and the Son and the Holy Spirit, teaching them to observe all that I commanded you; and lo, I am with you always, even to the end of the age."

If you are living by faith as one who is known as part of the Lord's family ("My People"), if by faith you are recognized as a holy person ("Holy People"), and if by faith you are actively engaged in "taking the land," spreading the gospel, teaching the truth, and interceding for the saints and the sinners (being a "Kingdom of Priests"), then you might already be a Milk and Honey Man.

Obstacles for the Israelites

In order for the sons of Israel to live in the Promised Land, they had to clear out the foreign nations. They had to acquire the land and to eliminate the influence of the false gods that had been in that land. In his messages near the end of the Israelites' pilgrimage, Moses told the people, "It is the LORD your God who is crossing over before you as a consuming fire. He will destroy them and he will subdue them before you so that you may drive them out and destroy them quickly, just as the LORD has spoken to you" (Deut. 9:3). Why would the Lord do this? "For they will turn your sons away from following Me to serve other gods" (Deut. 7:4).

In his last message to the Israelites, Moses said, "It is the LORD your God who will cross ahead of you; He will destroy these nations before you, and you shall dispossess them" (Deut. 31:3). In his farewell address, Joshua reported, "You have seen all that the LORD your God has done to all these nations because of you, for the LORD your God is He who has been fighting for you" (Josh. 23:3). Joshua also added a warning to obey the Mosaic law, "so that you will not associate with these nations [which could be translated 'Gentiles'], these which remain among you, or mention the name of their gods, or make anyone swear by them, or serve them, or bow down to them" (Josh. 23:7).

These nations represented a threat and an obstacle to the holiness of the sons of Israel. This had happened to them at Moab, when they had relations with the Moabite women and 23,000 (or 24,000) of them died (1 Cor. 10:8; Num. 25:1).

Obstacles for Us

All of us encounter obstacles when attempting to live the milk and honey life. Let's look at a few of them:

1. **Refusing to forgive.** The failure to forgive can be a significant obstacle in living a milk and honey life. Unforgiveness produces bitterness. When I was a pastor, a woman who lived more than fifty miles from our church came to me for counseling. She had been raped by a friend of the family at age nine. As is common, she had held a bitter grudge against the offender for quite a while. When I met her, she was a mother of young children, and she had carried that bitterness around. That was understandable. However, she had heard Christian counseling on the radio that taught her she needed to forgive the offender. She did, and as a result she was healed of her bitterness.

   By the time she came to me, she was experiencing some kind of emotional stress, and she could not figure out the source. My goal was to help her uncover where this stress was coming from. I helped her revisit her childhood, and when she did she recalled that a family member had molested her at the age of five. The incident of the rape she had experienced at age nine had been so dominant in her life that it had overshadowed the other incident. When the root of the current stress was revealed, she knew what to do. She forgave the earlier offender, and she was set free.

   In Matthew 6:14–15, Jesus said, "If you forgive men when they sin against you, your heavenly Father will also forgive you. But if you do not forgive men their sins, your Father will not forgive your sins." If we continue to harbor bitterness against those who have wronged us, it will plague us. However, if we recognize the problem and forgive others, we will gain freedom.

2. **Refusing to apologize.** Repentance is the flip side of forgiveness. In the matter of forgiveness, it is the other party that is the perpetrator of the problem. With repentance, however, we are the perpetrators who need to be forgiven.

   In Matthew 5:23–24, Jesus said, "If you are presenting your offering at the altar, and there remember that your brother has something against you, leave your offering there before the altar and go; first be reconciled to your brother, and then come and present your offering." Failure to make amends with your brother can block your worship of God and affect your relationship with Him. Failure to apologize to our children teaches them the wrong lesson—apologizing for the mistakes we have made gives them an example to follow.

3. **Participating in cults and the occult.** Some Christians have past experience with worship of false gods and involvement in Satanism, Tarot card reading, palm reading, etc. Whatever we have done in the past can still be "in our system." It can even be carried forward generationally from our ancestors. This can be a real obstacle to living victoriously—living as a Milk and Honey Man.

4. **Bondage.** Bondage is a specific reference to addictions in which our culture engages, such as addiction to drugs, alcohol, etc. These, too, can stand in the way of us living by faith and having Christ live His life through us.

The Victorious Spirit-filled Life

Overcoming these obstacles is something that you do for God's kingdom. When you get past these barriers, your life (and God's kingdom) will be better—it will taste like honey. Note that while you must follow through with the biblical injunctions and deal with these matters, it is not your flesh to which you are looking for victory, but the Spirit of God. Christ in you is the hope of glory.

There are some Christians who say, "Because Jesus is supposed to do the work, I will just sit in my recliner, watch television, and wait for groceries to come through the door and for dinner to be served." They have a mistaken view of the Spirit-filled life. That is not what Scripture teaches. Even though we rest in Christ, the Bible also directs that "if anyone is not willing to work, then He is not to eat either" (2 Thess. 3:10).

Take the Land

Remember, the events of the Israelites' pilgrimage from Egypt and the taking of the Promised Land happened to them as an example for us. God said, "Every place on which the sole of your foot treads, I have given it to you, just as I spoke to Moses" (Josh. 1:3). For this generation of the sons of Israel, whatever part they set foot on was given to them and was theirs to occupy. The whole land had been given to them for ownership. "From the wilderness and this Lebanon, even as far as the great river, the river Euphrates, all the land of the Hittites, and as far as the Great Sea [the Mediterranean] toward the setting of the sun, will be your territory" (v. 4).

Note that this would occur one step at a time, not all at once. It would happen on God's timetable. (In fact, to this day, the Israelites never have occupied as far as the Euphrates River.) In addition, the Israelites could only possess the land that they pursued. They could only possess the places where they "put their foot"; the territories they went to for the purpose of conquest.

The things that happened to the sons of Israel were examples for us in the twenty-first century on how to live Christ-centered lives. It is about changing the lives of individual Christians. It is about Christ as Life, the Milk and Honey Life, the Abundant Christian Life, the Exchanged Life, the Spirit-filled Life, the Victorious Life, or whatever term you use. It is about the milk and honey life.

The greatest saint is the greatest receiver. You have been given everything at salvation, but you can only use that which you pursue by faith. Study the Bible, continue to grow in your knowledge of what it means to be a Spirit-filled Christian, and then put your foot there and test it out. Is it true? Did Christ really provide that for you? What does that promise include? Go there.

Yes, you will face obstacles—including what you will perceive as unanswered prayer. God's Word says nothing can stop faith in action, and God's Word is always true and reliable. "No man will be able to stand before you all the days of your life. Just as I have been with Moses, I will be with you; I will not fail you or forsake you" (Josh. 1:5). Moses said something similar in Deuteronomy 31:6, and it was reiterated in the New Testament in Hebrews 13:5.

The sons of Israel followed the pillar of cloud by day and the pillar of fire by night. That was a visible indication of God's presence with them. Now we are told that even without this visible presence, God will be with us. Christians can be confident of Christ's presence.

Living in the Land of Milk and Honey

Jesus is "the way, and the truth, and the life" (John 14:6). Understand it, believe it, act upon it. He is life! Let Him be the Life in you. When you recognize that you have some obstacles and you seek to eliminate those obstacles through the Lord, you have passed another milestone. Once again, if you have crossed the three thresholds, please let me know and I will celebrate with you as you taste the milk and honey.

Appendix
Biblical Uses of *Psuche* (Soul)

THERE ARE VARIOUS ways to understand the make-up of man: Monochotomy (often called Monism), Dichotomy, and Trichotomy.

I.   Translations of *psuche* (soul) in the New American Standard Bible

    A. everyone (1 use)   F. person (1 use)

    B. heart (1 use)   G. persons (3 uses)

    C. life (36 uses)   H. soul (1 use)

    D. lives (7 uses)   I. souls (14 uses)

    E. mind (1 use)   J. thing (1 use)

II. *Psuche* can mean all of man or just parts of man
    A. It can mean the whole person (monochotomy)
        1. Romans 13:1: "Every person is to be in subjection to the governing authorities."
        2. 1 Peter 3:20: "A few, that is, eight persons, were brought safely through the water."
        3. Acts 7:14: "Joseph … invited … all his relatives to come to him, seventy-five persons in all."

B. It can mean the immaterial part of man (dichotomy)
1. Matthew 10:28: "Fear Him who is able to destroy both soul and body in hell."
2. 3 John 2: "Beloved, I pray that in all respects you may prosper and be in good health, just as your soul prospers."
3. Luke 2:34–35: "Simon ... said to Mary ... a sword will pierce even your own soul—to the end that thoughts from many hearts may be revealed."

C. It can mean a third part of man (trichotomony)
1. 1 Thessalonians 5:23: "May your spirit and soul and body be preserved complete."
2. Hebrews 4:12: "The Word of God is living and active and sharper than a two-edged sword, piercing as far as the division of soul and spirit."

III. The flesh (a combination of the body and the soul) and the Spirit
A. Galatians 5:19–21: "The deeds of the flesh ['sinful nature' in the NIV] are evident, which are: immorality, impurity, sensuality, idolatry, sorcery, enmities, strife, jealousy, outbursts of anger, disputes, dissensions, factions, envyings [in the soul part of the flesh], drunkenness [in the body part of the flesh], carousings ..."
B. Galatians 5:22–23: "The fruit [singular] of the Spirit is love, joy, peace, patience, kindness, goodness, faithfulness, gentleness, self-control." If you see a Christian manifesting just one of these items (for instance, patience), then he is simply a Christian with patience. If you see a Christian with all nine items, however, he is Spirit-filled. If you see a Christian manifest eight of the nine items, he has a lot of good flesh, but he is not Spirit-filled, because the fruit [singular] includes all nine items.

List of Spiritual Life Books
that are Christ-as-Life Related

THE FOLLOWING ARE books that teach the depth of the Christian life. I do not necessarily agree with all of the theology or the terminology used in these books, but I do believe that they contribute to the understanding of a Christian experiencing Christ-as-Life.

Core Books

If there are only seven books to be read to understand the message of "Christ in you, the hope of glory" (or "Christ as Life," "The Exchanged Life," "The Spirit-Filled Life," "The Abundant Life," "The Milk and Honey Life," "The Victorious Life" or "Union with Christ") the following are the seven I would recommend:

Anderson, Neil T. Christian *Victory Over the Darkness: Realizing the Power of Your Identity in Christ.* Ventura, CA: Regal Books, a division of Gospel Light, 2000, 239 pp. This book will help you realize the power of knowing your identity in Christ, free yourself from bondage to the "garbage" in your past, and stand against the spiritual forces of darkness.

George, Bob. *Classic Christianity: Life's Too Short to Miss the Real Thing.* Eugene, OR: Harvest House Publishers, 1989, 205 pp. Bob, a business-man, received Christ at age thirty-six and went into the ministry, where he soon burned out. He then learned what the resurrection was all about. Bob has a radio-counseling ministry and held a one-night, evangelistic meeting in our home in Dallas at Christmas in 1976.

Gillham, Bill, EdD. *Lifetime Guarantee: Making Your Christian Life Work and What to Do When It Doesn't.* Brentwood, TN: Wolgemuth & Hyatt Publishers, 1987, 227 pp. This book is by a counselor to pastors. His term "earthsuit" helped my understanding of this concept.

McVey, Steve. *Grace Walk: What You've Always Wanted in the Christian Life.* Eugene, OR: Harvest House Publishers, 1995, 188 pp. This is a superb book on the concept of Christ-as-Life and the understanding of grace in our lives. Highly recommended!

Nee, Watchman. *The Normal Christian Life,* Wheaton, IL: Tyndale House Publishers, first published in India in 1957, 285 pp. This is a great Christian classic. Beginning in the 1930s, Nee helped establish local churches in China without the help of any foreign missionary organizations.

Solomon, Charles R. *Handbook to Happiness: A Guide to Victorious Living and Effective Counseling.* Wheaton, IL: Tyndale House Publishers, 1971, 152 pp. I learned about the exchanged life through this ministry.

Stone, Dan and David Gregory. *The Rest of the Gospel: When the Partial Gospel Has Worn You Out).* Corvallis, OR: One Press, 2000, 254 pp. *The Rest of the Gospel* is based on the concept that we have incomplete knowledge of what took place on the cross. It is not just that Jesus died for our sin, but also that Jesus died to sin and we died with Him.

Additional Resources

If you can't get enough of this subject, here are a few additional books that I would recommend.

Anderson, Neil T. *Living Free in Christ: The Truth About Who You Are and How Christ Can Meet Your Deepest Needs.* Ventura, CA: Gospel Light, 1993, 312 pp. Anderson says, "It is not what we do that determines who we are. It is who we are that determines what we do. I am burdened for those who have never discovered their identity in Christ nor the freedom He brings."

Anderson, Neil T. *The Bondage Breaker: Overcoming Negative Thoughts, Irrational Feelings, Habitual Sins.* Eugene, OR: Harvest House Publishers, 1993, 276 pp. This book explains our position of freedom, protection and authority in Christ; warns of susceptibility in Christ; and gives steps to freedom in Christ. Anderson offers many profitable books for understanding freedom in Christ.

Edman, V. Raymond. *They Found the Secret: Twenty Transformed Lives That Reveal a Touch of Eternity.* Grand Rapids, MI: Zondervan Publishing House, 1960, 1984, 192 pp. This book is made up of short presentations of the lives of twenty saints who experienced victory in the Christian life. Several of the featured individuals use (incorrectly, from my point of view) the term "baptized in the Holy Spirit." This book can help us realize the subject of victory is across the doctrinal lines as well as the years.

Feazel, D. Kerlin. *Not Sinners After All.* Shippensburg, PA: Treasure House, 1994, 170 pp. This book touches on part of the subject of our identity in Christ. I have not heard of any other books as focused on this subject as this one is focused.

Huntsperger, Larry. *The Grace Exchange: God's Offer of Freedom from a Life of Works.* Eugene, OR: Harvest House Publishers, 1995. Huntsperger, a student of Francis Schaeffer at L'Abri Fellowship in Switzerland, is another who has discovered the reality of the life of God's Spirit flowing through us. He describes two deadly swamps: moral disobedience and man-made religion. He teaches the secrets to freedom overcoming doubts, insecurities, and how to experience spiritual fulfillment.

McMillen, S. I. and David E. Stern. *None of These Diseases: The Bible's Health Secrets for the 21st Century.* Grand Rapids, MI: Fleming H. Revell, revised edition 2000, 285 pp. Based on Exodus 15:26, the subject of this book is the same as that of Chapter 8 in *The Milk and Honey Man.*

Murray, Andrew. *Absolute Surrender (and Other Addresses).* Chicago, IL: Moody Press, 127 pp. Murray was one of the most well-known spiritual life preachers of 100 years ago. The title of this book is that of the first chapter, which is the reason why I recommend it. Other spiritual life messages include "Having Begun in the Spirit."

Murray, Andrew. *The Power of the Blood of Christ.* New Kensington, PA: Whitaker House, 1993. Written by a well known nineteenth-century African pastor, "This mighty weapon of spiritual warfare holds the secret to a victorious life."

Nee, Watchman. *The Release of the Spirit.* Cloverdale, IN: Ministry of Life/ Sure Foundation Publishers, 1965, 94 pp. Brother Nee has clearly seen the absolute necessity of brokenness. He believes the breaking of soul-powers is imperative if the human spirit is to express the life of the Lord Jesus.

Needham, David. *Birthright: Christian, Do You Know Who You Are?* Portland, OR: Multnomah Press, 1979, 293 pp. This was the first book I read that challenged the common concept of "sin nature," that questioned who we are ("to enter the kingdom of God requires that one be of a different species!"), and that pointed out that saying "no" to all of our desires does not guarantee we will be holy.

Taylor, Dr. Howard and Mrs. Howard Taylor. *Hudson Taylor's Spiritual Secret.* Chicago, IL: Moody Press, 1932, 253 pp. J. Hudson Taylor, the founder of China Inland Ministry, served as a missionary in China and, after some time in that endeavor, experienced the joy of "the Exchanged Life" (Chapter 14 in this book). This book reveals Taylor's true source of his unusual and extraordinary power.

Taylor, Jack R. *The Key to Triumphant Living: An Adventure in Personal Discovery.* Nashville, TN: Broadman Press, 1971, 160 pp. This book contains graphics on the makeup of man and specific treatment of the self-life.

Thomas, Major Ian. *The Saving Life of Christ: Help to New Converts and Defeated Christians.* Grand Rapids, MI: Zondervan Publishing House, 1961, 143 pp. Major Thomas found the truth at age nineteen, and during his life has seen many pastors and Sunday school teachers who were not living the full, joyous life in Christ. This book includes many types from the Egypt to Canaan Pilgrimage in the Old Testament.

Unknown Christian. *How to Live the Victorious Life.* Grand Rapids, MI: Zondervan Publishing House, 1960, 1986, 109 pp. This book "nudges believers beyond complacency and on to godliness."

Endnotes

Chapter 1

1. John F. Walvoord and Roy B. Zuck, editors, *The Bible Knowledge Commentary*, Old Testament (Wheaton, IL: Victor Books, 1985), Chart of the Plagues and the Gods and Goddesses of Egypt, p. 120 (with personal modifications).
2. Dr. Charles R. Solomon, *Handbook to Happiness* (Wheaton, IL: Tyndale House Publishers, Inc., 1971).
3. J. D. Douglas, organizing editor, *The New Bible Dictionary*, (Grand Rapids, MI: Wm. B. Eerdmans, 1962), "milk," p. 822.
4. Merrill C. Tenney, *Zondervan Pictorial Encyclopedia of the Bible*, vol. 3 (Grand Rapids, MI: Zondervan, 1977), pp. 196–197.
5. Merrill Unger, *Unger's Bible Dictionary* (Chicago, IL: Moody Press, 1966), p. 497. Canaan is often described in the Old Testament as a land "flowing with milk and honey" (Ex. 3:8, 17). This graphic figure of speech portrays the fertile land supplying rich pasturage for cattle, which give such abundant milk the land is said to flow with it, and producing many kinds of flowers, giving food to honey-producing bees. The Word of God is compared with honey as spiritually delectable (see Ps. 19:10; 119:103).
6. Douglas, *The New Bible Dictionary*, p. 822. In some places, milk stands alone as a symbol of prosperity and abundance (see Isa. 60:16; Joel 3:18).

Chapter 2

7. Mary was a virgin and was "overshadowed" by the Holy Spirit (Luke 1:35); therefore, Jesus had no earthly father. Life is in the blood (Lev. 17:11), and because blood is not transmitted through the umbilical cord from the mother to the baby, Jesus did not get blood from Mary. He is described as being "born of a woman" in Galatians 4:4.
8. The "flesh" is translated "sinful nature" in the *New International Version*.
9. See the appendix for a study of the New Testament use of Soul (*psuche*).

Chapter 3

10. John F. Walvoord and Roy B. Zuck, editors, *The Bible Knowledge Commentary*, Old Testament (Wheaton, IL: Victor Books, 1985), Chart of the Plagues and the Gods and Goddesses of Egypt, p. 120 (with personal modifications).

False God	False God	Possible "Power" of Plague from the Lord	Reference	Application
Hapi – Nile River	agriculture	Nile turned into blood	Exodus 7:14–25	economy, provision of food
Heqt Frogs	goddess of birth	frogs covered the land	Exodus 8:1–15	heritage
Set	god of the desert, cleanliness	gnats/lice on all men and animals	Exodus 8:16–19	pride
Uatchit		swarms of flies	Exodus 8:20–32	
Apis, Hathor (cow head)	cattle, beasts of burden	pestilence on Egyptian cows (they died)	Exodus 9:1–7	source of labor, Egyptian economy
Sekhmet- Sunu- Isis-	disease pestilence healing	boils	Exodus 9:8–12	health
Nut- Set- Osiris	the sky storms crops	hail	Exodus 9:13–35	crops
Osiris	crops	locusts ate plants and fruit	Exodus 10:1–20	crops

Ra	sun	three days of darkness	Exodus 10:21–29	light
Isis	protected children	death of firstborn	Exodus 11:1–12:30	heritage

11. Merrill C. Tenney and Steven Barbas, editors, *The Zondervan Pictorial Encyclopedia of the Bible*, vol. 4 (Grand Rapids, MI: Zondervan Publishing House, 1975), p. 437.

12. "Hapi (Hapy)," Ancient Egypt: The Mythology, http://www.egyptian-myths.net/hapi.htm.

13. John MacArthur, *The MacArthur Study Bible* (Nashville, TN: Thomas Nelson, 1997), Exodus 7:15, footnote, p. 103.

14. Walvoord and Zuck, *The Bible Knowledge Commentary*, "Exodus," by John D. Hannah, p. 122.

15. Merrill F. Unger, *Unger's Bible Dictionary* (Chicago, IL: Moody Press, 1966), p. 870.

16. Walvoord and Zuck, *The Bible Knowledge Commentary*, p. 122.

17. Frank E Gabelein, general editor, *The Expositor's Bible Commentary* (Grand Rapids, MI: Zondervan Corporation, 1990), "Exodus," by Walter C. Kaiser, Jr., p. 355.

18. "Hathor," Egyptian Dreams, http://www.egyptiandreams.co.uk/hathor.php.

19. "Sekhmet," Wikipedia, http://en.wikipedia.org/wiki/Sekhmet.

Chapter 4

20. Bill Gillham, EdD., *Lifetime Guarantee: Making Your Christian Life Work and What to Do When It Doesn't*, (Brentwood, TN: Wolgemuth & Hyatt, Publishers, 1987).

21. Bob George, *Classic Christianity* (Eugene, OR: Harvest House Publishers, Inc., 1989).

Chapter 7

22. Merrill C. Tenney and Steven Barbas, editors, *The Zondervan Pictorial Encyclopedia of the Bible*, vol. 1 (Grand Rapids, MI: Zondervan Publishing House, 1975), s.v. "assurance," by J. Daane, p. 371.

23. These are very brief presentations of evidence of the fact that the Bible is true. For many more reasons and expansion of the evidence of these two reasons, it is recommended that you read Josh McDowell and Bill Wilson, *A Ready Defense* (San Bernardino, CA: Here's Life Publishers, Inc., 1990).

Chapter 8

24. S. I. McMillen, M.D. and David E. Stern, M.D., *None of These Diseases* (Grand Rapids, MI: Fleming H. Revell, 2000), p. 13.
25. Ibid, pp. 17, 18, 267.
26. Ibid, pp. 30–31.
27. Ibid, pp. 45–47.
28. N. E. Whitehead, Ph.D., "Homosexuality and Mental Health Problems," http://www.narth.com/docs/whitehead.html.
29. McMillen and Stern, *None of These Diseases*, p. 179.
30. Ibid, p. 212.
31. Ibid, p. 213.
32. Gary R. Collins, Ph.D., *Christian Counseling* (Waco, TX: Word Books, 1980), p. 100.
33. Ibid, p. 205.
34. McMillen and Stern, *None of These Diseases*, p. 216.
35. Ibid, p. 262. While this book does not set out to specifically teach the reader how to make Christ his life, nevertheless this portion of the book is part of the instruction on Christ as life.

Chapter 10

36. Charles C. Ryrie, *The Ryrie Study Bible, New American Standard Bible* (Chicago, IL: Moody Bible Institute, 1978), annotation at John 7:37–39, p. 1615.

Chapter 11

37. See chapter 13 on "The Mosaic Law."

Chapter 12

38. Grace Fellowship International, 3914 Nellie Street, P. O. Box 368, Pigeon Forge, TN, 37868, (865) 429–0450, www.GraceFellowshipIntl. com.

Chapter 15

39. "Trust and Obey," words by John H. Sammis, tune by Daniel B. Towner, *Baptist Hymnal*, (Nashville, TN: Convention Press, 1975), p. 409.
40. Backing up to Numbers 10:11, we find that the Israelites' march to Kadesh-Barnea began on the twentieth day of the second month of the second year. The time spent traveling, grumbling, and spying out the land for forty days would total about four months.
41. "The widespread view that he was concerned about mere professors of the faith as over against genuine believers is not found in the text." John F. Walvoord and Roy B. Zuck, *The Bible Knowledge Commentary* (Wheaton, IL: Victor Books, 1983), "Hebrews" by Zane Hodges, p. 787.
42. Taken from *The Saving Life of Christ* by Major W. Ian Thomas. Copyright © 1961 by Zondervan Publishing House, pp. 7–9. Used by permission of Zondervan.
43. Dr. Steve McVey, *Grace Walk* (Eugene, OR: Harvest House Publishers, 1995), p. 11. This is a great book that teaches Christ-as-Life by the president of Grace Walk Ministries, a discipleship-training ministry in Atlanta, Georgia.
44. Bob George, *Classic Christianity* (Eugene, OR: Harvest House Publishers, 1989), p. 23.

Chapter 16

45. Dr. Roy B. Zuck, *Basic Bible Interpretation* (Wheaton, IL: Victor Books, 1991), p. 174.
46. Deuteronomy 3:11 notes that Og was a king with a king-sized bed—it was 13½ feet long by 6 feet wide and made of iron.

Chapter 18

47. This is possibly a term for the early Moabites. See Frank E. Gabelein, general editor, *The Expositors Bible Commentary*, vol. 2 (Grand Rapids, MI: Zondervan Publishing House, 1990), "Numbers," by Ronald B. Allen, pp. 910–911.

Chapter 19

48. The land where Abraham settled is called the land of Canaan (Gen. 13:12).
49. Jack R. Taylor, *The Key to Triumphant Living* (Nashville, TN: Broadman Press, 1971), p. 35.
50. Bill Gilliam, quoted in the foreword to *Grace Walk* by Dr. Steve McVey (Eugene, OR: Harvest House Publishers, 1995).
51. Dr. Charles R. Solomon, *Handbook to Happiness* (Wheaton, IL: Tyndale House, 1999), p. 51.
52. Ibid. p. 73.
53. There are Scripture verses that describe Christ being in us and others that describe the Holy Spirit being in us. First John 3:24 is helpful: "We know by this that He abides in us, by the Spirit whom He has given us."

Chapter 20

54. Medical benefits of circumcision include a decreased risk of urinary tract infections, a reduced risk of sexually transmitted diseases, a reduced risk of cervical cancer in female sex partners, and other benefits. See Tracy C. Shuman, M.D., ed., "Sexual Health: Circumcision," WebMD, February 1, 2006, http://www.webmd.com/sexual-conditions/guide/circumcision.

Chapter 21

55. The capitals in this verse are from the Scripture (it is quoting the Old Testament).